STUPID ON THE ROAD

Other Books by Leland Gregory

What's the Number for 911?

What's the Number for 911 Again?

The Stupid Crook Book

Hey, Idiot!

Idiots at Work

Bush-Whacked

Idiots in Love

Am-Bushed!

Stupid History

Idiots in Charge

Cruel and Unusual Idiots

What's the Number for 911? Second Edition

Stupid American History

Stupid Science

Stupid California

Stupid Texas

STUPID
ON THE ROAD

Idiots on Planes, Trains, Buses, and Cars

LELAND GREGORY

Andrews McMeel Publishing, LLC

Kansas City • Sydney • London

10 11 12 13 14 RR2 10 9 8 7 6 5 4 3 2 1

ISBN-13: 978-0-7407-7913-8
ISBN-10: 0-7407-7913-3

Library of Congress Control Number: 2009940825

Book design by Holly Camerlinck
Illustrations by Robert Mag

www.andrewsmcmeel.com

Attention: Schools and Businesses
Andrews McMeel books are available at quantity discounts with bulk purchase for educational, business, or sales promotional use. For information, please write to: Special Sales Department, Andrews McMeel Publishing, LLC, 1130 Walnut Street, Kansas City, Missouri 64106.

STUPID ON THE ROAD

LOCO-MOTIVE

It was referred to as "the train from hell," and it had its 109 passengers railing against Amtrak. It was supposed to be a happy journey from Chicago to Seattle, but the conductors couldn't keep the train's schedule on track. First there was the onboard drug bust in Wisconsin, and then the train hit an abandoned car on the tracks in Minnesota. Soon a faulty indicator light delayed the trip just long enough for a blizzard to really slow things down (so much so that the train ran low on fuel). Next, a drunken father and son got into a fight shortly before the tracks were blocked by a derailed freight train. To make matters worse, the train ran out of food and was forced to wait for a Kentucky Fried Chicken delivery in Spokane. The train eventually rumbled into the Seattle station on its last legs (well, there was a wing and a thigh left, too) twelve hours behind schedule. The entire trip took fifty-seven hours and brought to mind the old World War II slogan "Is this trip really necessary?"

Insurance Files
PART ONE

The following are actual statements given by insurance policyholders describing automobile accidents in which they were involved.

"The other car collided with mine without giving warning of its intention."

"I thought my window was down but found it was up when I put my hand through it."

"A pedestrian hit me and went under my car."

"The guy was all over the place. I had to swerve a number of times before I hit him."

"I pulled away from the side of the road, glanced at my mother-in-law, and headed over the embankment."

ROAD RAGE
TO ROAD RASH

Stephen Thomas Manley, Jr., was driving down Farm Road 920 north of Weatherford, Texas, when a car driven by B. J. Justin Lundin began tailgating him. Manley tapped his brakes to get Lundin to back off, an action that apparently enraged the twenty-year-old Poolville, Texas, native. According to an article in the *Fort Worth Star-Telegram*, Lundin passed Manley on the night of January 6, 2003, and then blocked his car by stopping in front of it. Lundin then jumped out of his car and began throwing rocks at Manley. He was in the process of kicking and hitting Manley's car when another car drove by and ran him over, killing him instantly.

"Text-Messaging Driver Hits Parked Patrol Car"

—*Arizona Republic* headline, June 27, 2007

ALIGHTED WITH SURPRISE

A malfunction during the switch-over from track power to overhead power lines prompted a conductor on a New York commuter train to stop and go up top with a fire extinguisher to investigate. According to a February 2008 article in the *White Plains (NY) Journal News*, it was fortunate that he took the fire extinguisher because the eleven to fourteen thousand volts of electricity surging through the overhead lines had caused a man, thirty-six-year-old Ricardo Chavez, to burst into flames up there. The conductor put out the torched train hopper, and Chavez was hospitalized in fair condition—no word, however, on why he was on top of the train to begin with.

Finishing thirty-fifth in the Club North Shore Half Marathon near Chicago in April 1993 was thirty-eight-year-old Mr. Farm Vehicle.

A PICTURE IS WORTH A THOUSAND WORDS

A lead-footed motorist was caught by a high-speed camera that photographed his car's license plate and recorded his speed. When police mailed the speeder his sixty-five-dollar ticket, they included the photograph that was imprinted with the date and speed. In response, the motorist mailed them a photograph of a check. Not wanting the photograph wars to develop any further, the police mailed the man a picture of a pair of handcuffs. He got the picture, in more ways than one, and immediately sent them a check for the full amount.

On March 27, 2003, the *Boulder (CO) Daily Camera* reported that a thirty-nine-year-old driver from Boulder had accidentally crashed into a tree after celebrating his car's odometer hitting one hundred thousand miles with a bottle of champagne.

GONE BUT NOT FORGOTTEN

A man in East Orange, New Jersey, was driving down I-280 on his way to work when a truck crossed the median and crushed the driver's side of his car. Rescue workers were able to extract the man using the Jaws of Life and, once he was freed, the man hitched a ride from a passing motorist and went to work. The event was reported on the news, and the man's wife saw the horrible accident, heard that the driver was missing, and assumed that her husband had died in the crash. She called local hospitals, the police, and the morgue, but no one knew where her husband was—until, that is, he walked through the door of their house. A coworker had given the man a ride home. When the entire ordeal sank in, the man went into a state of shock and took the next three days off from work.

THE SCALES OF JUSTICE

Two Florida police officers decided to follow the operator of a car because he was driving like he was a little green. They tailed the car for nearly two miles before pulling it over and discovering the driver *was* green—he was an iguana. When the officers approached the car, they noticed a three-and-a-half-foot iguana at the wheel and an intoxicated John Ruppell slouched down in the driver's seat. The iguana didn't have car insurance but was friends with the gecko from the Geico commercials.

VIOLATION $100.00

No. 9

Month	Day	Year	City	State

Plate No.		VIN		Expiration date

Name	Location

A twenty-five-year-old woman in Mount Prospect, Illinois, lost the toes on her right foot when she decided to crawl under a slow-moving train as a shortcut from one platform to another.

Signature	Officer No.

WHAT'S THE BIG BEEF?

A lot of things can hit your windshield while driving, but one Austrian woman really had a cow when she saw what had struck her windshield—it was a cow. According to the Austria Press Agency, in June 2002, a thirty-six-year-old woman was injured after a cow fell and landed on the hood of her car. The cow's fatal fall occurred after it had strayed from a hillside onto the flat roof of a tunnel, lost its hoofing, and plummeted just as the car emerged from the tunnel. The woman's car quickly went from cloth seats to all leather upholstery.

"Wienermobile: Contestants Relish the Thought"

—Wisconsin State Journal headline, June 1, 2004

GREASED MONKEY

A man left the Go-Go-Rama bar on Route 35 in New Jersey, got into his vintage Mustang, and turned the key, but the car wouldn't start. He knew the starter was faulty so he pulled out an old screwdriver and popped the hood. Knowing just enough about cars to be dangerous, the man used the screwdriver to create an arc across the solenoid, giving the starter the jolt of electricity it needed to turn the engine over. The trick worked like a charm, but unfortunately the man wasn't living a charmed life—he had left the car in gear. As soon as the engine cranked up, the car lurched forward and drove over both a fifteen-foot embankment and its owner—making him one of those rare people who have actually run themselves over with their own cars.

WHAT DOES THE GAS PEDAL DO?

Police thought the driver of an armored truck in Edmonton, Alberta, was trying to signal them for help by repeatedly opening and closing the truck's door. Calling for backup, the original officer and five other patrol cars pulled the armored car over to find out the true nature of the problem. It turned out there wasn't an emergency; the driver was simply trying to fan fresh air into the cab after his partner had passed gas.

VIOLATION $100.00

No. 13

Month	Day	Year	City	State

Plate No.		VIN	Expiration date

Name	Location

According to the 1991 police log in the
Muskego (WI) Sun, twenty-two-year-old
Rhonda L. Stipe was injured in April when,
while driving on the road, she "ran into a
19-ton pile of gravel."

Signature	Officer No.

DRIVEN TO DISTRACTION

A young female student in Durham, North Carolina, was behind the wheel of a car with her driver's education instructor when another car cut them off. The teacher, David Cline, ordered the young woman to "Follow that car!" And she did. They soon caught up with the offending car, and Cline jumped out and started punching the driver. Police let the student driver drive off but instructed the instructor that he was under arrest. Cline was later released on a four-hundred-dollar bond.

In Nice, France, a woman was injured when she accidentally drove her car off a thirty-foot cliff. The woman was in a hurry to go home to tell her family the good news that she had recently been hired as a driving instructor.

Insurance Files
PART TWO

The following are actual statements given by insurance policyholders describing automobile accidents in which they were involved.

"The accident occurred when I was attempting to bring my car out of a skid by steering into the other vehicle."

"I was driving my car out the driveway in the usual manner when it was struck by the other car in the same place it had been struck several times before."

"I was on my way to the doctor's with rear-end trouble when my universal joint gave way causing me to have an accident."

"As I approached the intersection, a stop sign suddenly appeared in a place where no stop sign had ever appeared before. I was unable to stop in time to avoid the accident."

A WEIGHTY SUBJECT

A woman called a travel agent and asked, "Do airlines put your physical description on your bag so they know whose luggage belongs to who?"

The agent replied, "No, why do you ask?"

The timid-sounding woman said, "Well, when I checked in with the airline, they put a tag on my luggage that said 'FAT,' and I'm overweight. Is there any connection?"

After putting the woman on hold for a minute while she regained her composure, the agent explained that the airport code for Fresno, California, is FAT, and that the airline was just putting a destination tag on her luggage. Makes you wonder: If the woman saw the word "terminal" on her luggage, would she have thought she was really sick?

THE YOUNG AND THE RESTLESS

Police in Fridley, Minnesota, pursued a 4 x 4 truck with speeds reaching 70 miles per hour until they were finally able to stop the speeder by bumping into the rear of the vehicle. A baby-sitter had reported the vehicle as stolen and identified the perpetrator as the ten-year-old boy she was watching. Police led the young boy, clad in *Lion King* pajamas, back to his home and notified his parents. After hearing about the incident, the boy's parents, I would guess, were ready to shorten his "circle of life."

An eleven-year-old boy from Kennett, Missouri, stole his parents' car and led police on a high-speed chase with speeds reaching 110 miles per hour.

THE CYCLE OF DRINKING

A forty-one-year-old Pittsburgh, Pennsylvania, man was arrested for riding a ten-speed bicycle while under the influence of alcohol. The man, Francis Glancy, never drives a car and doesn't have a driver's license but was ordered to obtain one just so the state could suspend it. Assistant Public Defender Tom Caulfield told reporters, "If he doesn't go and get a driver's license, he's gonna end up with a criminal record." Glancy, who registered a 0.328 blood-alcohol level, was arrested after he suffered minor injuries from falling off his bicycle. If Glancy doesn't cooperate with the authorities, he'll go from bars to handlebars to behind bars.

An officer approached the driver of a car he had pulled over for speeding, and the man gave a very convincing excuse: "My wife is ovulating," he told the officer. "I have to get home right now."

ACCIDENTS BY DESIGN

Matthew Geraci suffered "severe brain damage" after a devastating automobile accident in 1989 in which he was struck by a car traveling in excess of 100 miles per hour. During rehabilitation, Geraci, who never expressed any passion or talent for artistic endeavors, suddenly began drawing. A July 14, 1994, article in the *Seattle Post-Intelligencer* described the now celebrated local artist's show of "colorful, abstract" fish that opened in a gallery in South Bend, Washington. In addition to his miraculous artistic talent, Geraci is now also a published author and poet. A neuropsychiatrist from the University of Washington was quoted as saying, "[There is] nothing in the [medical] literature" to explain Geraci's condition.

"Police: Man Runs Over Wife After 'Who Drives' Spat"

—*Florida Today* headline, February 22, 2008

THE SUPERIOR RACE

In August 1993, three Tarahumara Indians from northern Mexico, one aged fifty-five, finished first, second, and fifth in the grueling one-hundred-mile "Leadville Trail 100: The Race Across the Sky." Runners compete along mountain roads and forest paths in the heart of the Colorado Rockies. The race, with its lowest point at 9,200 feet and its highest point, Hope Pass, at 12,600 feet, is the highest altitude race in the United States. Not only did the three Indians finish first, second, and fifth, they were also the only runners not wearing conventional running shoes—they wore huaraches, homemade sandals made out of old tire treads and leather straps.

WHITE-LINE FEVER

The following are real answers received on exams given by the California Department of Transportation's driving school:

Q: Do you yield when a blind pedestrian is crossing the road?

A: What for? He can't see my license plate.

Q: Who has the right of way when four cars approach a four-way stop at the same time?

A: The pickup truck with the gun rack and the bumper sticker saying, "Guns don't kill people. I do."

Q: When driving through fog, what should you use?

A: Your car.

Q: What changes would occur in your lifestyle if you could no longer drive lawfully?

A: I would be forced to drive unlawfully.

CANINE CRUISER

The headline could have read "Man Dies When Dog Hits Hog." An unidentified thirty-nine-year-old man was riding his motorcycle on U.S. 85 in Commerce City, Colorado, when it started raining cats and dogs—well, actually it rained just one dog. The forty-pound mutt toppled off an overhead railroad bridge and landed on the unsuspecting motorcyclist. The man tried doggedly to maintain control of his bike during the July 1994 incident, but he spun out and crashed into an oncoming truck.

"Man Drives Home with Headless Friend"
—Associated Press headline, August 31, 2004

THREE'S COMPANY, TOO

On February 5, 2002, Arkansas secretary of state Bill McCuen pleaded guilty to felony charges that he took bribes, evaded taxes, and accepted kickbacks. The report also mentioned the ethical questioning McCuen received in November 1991 when he was asked about taking two female employees on what he referred to as a "business trip" to Las Vegas. McCuen claimed he took two ladies to avoid any appearance of impropriety that might have arisen from taking only one. He also explained that three people could travel almost as cheaply as one—especially if they all shared the same motel room, as they did while traveling through Gallup, New Mexico.

NOT ENOUGH HORSE SENSE

A police officer in Middlefield, Ohio, spotted a vehicle heading down a stretch of road with the driver fast asleep. The officer gave chase while trying to get the driver to wake up and regain control of the vehicle. The police officer didn't turn on his siren, though, because he didn't want to spook the horse. You see, the driver was a seventeen-year-old Amish boy and the vehicle was his horse-drawn carriage. The officer blocked the road with his cruiser, and the horse, buggy, and rider all careened into a ditch. The horse was slightly injured but made a full recovery. The boy was charged with DUI.

YOU CHEEKY GIRL

Thirty-two-year-old Tamara Jo Klemkowsky of Waldorf, Maryland, suffered several broken bones and was hospitalized in April 1994 after she fell out the emergency window of a chartered party bus traveling 55 miles per hour. Klemkowsky accidentally caused the window to open after she dropped her pants and mooned a passing automobile.

AN ACCIDENT WAITING TO HAPPEN

Lynne F. Herron was fired as a municipal train driver in Cleveland, Ohio, after she deliberately deactivated a safety system that led to an accident that injured fourteen people. Because of a labor contract requirement with the Regional Transit Authority, Herron, thirty-three, was immediately rehired as a municipal bus driver.

"Chariot Race Death Probed"

—*Toronto Star* headline, August 3, 2004

THAT STORY TAKES THE CAKE

A March 24, 2008, Associated Press article reported that a Connecticut state trooper pulled over Justin Vonkummer of Millerton, New York, for driving his 1993 BMW over the speed limit. Vonkummer told the officer that he wasn't a drunken driver but that he was a dunk driver—he had been dunking an Oreo cookie into a cup of milk when it slipped through his fingers. The cop listened as the man told him that while he was fishing out "America's Favorite Cookie" he accidentally accelerated. Vonkummer was also charged with driving on a suspended license.

In May 1996, a former flight attendant for USAir was sentenced to eight months in prison for forcing a plane to land by calling in a bomb threat so she could rest her injured knee.

THAT'S NOT MANNA FROM HEAVEN

Bob Ringewold and a friend were driving in Holland, Michigan, in June 1996 when something slammed into the roof of his car. He pulled over to see what it was and was surprised to find the dent was caused by a five-pound sucker fish that had simply fallen from the sky. Apparently, an eagle flying overhead had lost its grip on the fish. Although Ringewold was upset with the dent in his roof, he was more than happy to take the fish home for dinner.

THE FLIGHT OF THE LIVING DEAD

You never know who you'll wind up sitting next to on a crowded airplane: the talkative type, the person who's afraid of flying, the airsick passenger, or worse. Well, one Canadian family complained to Continental Airlines because they were stuck with the worst kind of passenger—a dead one. After a sick passenger, hooked up to IVs and oxygen, foamed at the mouth and died during an April 2001 flight across the Pacific, he was kept in his seat for the rest of the five-hour trip.

VIOLATION

$100.00

No. 33

Month	Day	Year	City	State

Plate No.		VIN	Expiration date

Name	Location

According to an August 13, 2001, article in the *Albany (OR) Democrat-Herald*, an eighteen-year-old man in Lebanon, Oregon, was killed as he was hanging out of a passenger-side car window. The driver of the vehicle came too close to a trash can, and the teenager fatally struck his head.

Signature	Officer No.

Insurance Files
PART THREE

The following are actual statements given by insurance policyholders describing automobile accidents in which they were involved.

"The telephone pole was approaching fast. I was attempting to swerve out of its path when it struck my front end."

"To avoid hitting the bumper of the car in front, I struck the pedestrian."

"My car was legally parked as it backed into the other vehicle."

"An invisible car came out of nowhere, struck my vehicle, and vanished."

"When I saw I could not avoid a collision, I stepped on the gas and crashed into the other car."

"The pedestrian had no idea which direction to go, so I ran him over."

SHE'S THE BOMB

A Royal Jordanian Airlines flight en route to Chicago in November 1996 was forced to land in Iceland after a bomb threat was phoned in. It was later discovered that the call was merely a ruse by a woman trying to keep her mother-in-law, a passenger on the plane, from visiting her in Chicago.

"Car Damaged by Flying Portable Toilet"
—Associated Press headline, June 10, 2004

A REAL CRAPPY PASSENGER

On October 20, 1995, thirty-seven-year-old Gerald Finneran of Greenwich, Connecticut, was arrested at JFK International Airport in New York as he disembarked from a United Airlines flight from Buenos Aires. According to an FBI report, Finneran, who began drinking before the flight, continued to demand more and more alcohol from flight attendants and was eventually cut off after he began helping himself to alcohol from the serving cart. Finneran became irate and assaulted a flight attendant and then dropped his pants and underwear and defecated on a serving cart (wiping himself with linen napkins). The pilot discontinued food service for fear of contamination, and first-class passengers had to suffer through the remaining four-hour flight with the pungent odor. The plane would have been rerouted earlier but one of the first-class passengers was Mário Alberto Nobre Lopes Soares, the president of Portugal, and regulations are stricter when there is a dignitary aboard.

A SIX-PACK OF PAIN

"I think where he was was the worst possible place to be," said the medical director of the Queensland, Australia, Ambulance Service. He was talking about the most unfortunate passenger of the six who were injured in a rear-end collision between a Ford Festiva and a larger car. So how can you fit six people in a tiny Festiva? You put one of them in the trunk, according to the *Brisbane Courier-Mail*. "It's literally too stupid for words," said a spokesman for the Royal Automobile Club of Queensland. "But we do feel badly for the man."

"**Defendant Stole Bicycle to Get to Court on Time**"
—*Guardian* headline, June 13, 2006

IMMEDIATE CAR PARTS

According to the *Kronen Zeitung* newspaper, in June 2003 an Austrian man walked up to his Ford Cougar, pulled out his keys, pushed the keyless entry remote, and watched as his car exploded. Police in the Austrian town of Sollenau originally investigated the event as a possible bomb attack but soon discovered that the cause was the owner's own actions. Apparently the man had two cylinders filled with oxyacetylene gas in his trunk, and the valves on both were slightly open. When he pushed the remote, a spark set off the gas and his Detroit steel became scrap metal.

TEEN DREAM

A mother who lives in Normandy Park, Washington, was concerned when she discovered that her thirteen-year-old son was missing on June 11, 2003. She soon realized that her son hadn't run away from home—he had flown away. The unidentified mother checked their home computer and discovered that her son had used her credit card to purchase an airline ticket to Maui. She notified the authorities, and a Maui officer met the boy as he disembarked from the plane and immediately put him on a return flight to Washington. Mom was unable to get a refund on the price of the ticket so she sentenced her high-flying flight risk to two years of yard work to cover her expenses.

"Law & Disorder: Woman, 38, Charged in Hit, Hit, Hit, Hit, Hit, Run"

—*Jacksonville (FL) Times-Union* headline, December 21, 2006

COLOR CORRECTION

Traffic Commissioner Matt Flynn of Laguna Beach, California, decided to dismiss a man's speeding ticket in October 1993 because the cop's motorcycle was the wrong color. According to state law, all police vehicles must be painted either black and white or just white—but this officer's motorcycle was painted blue and white.

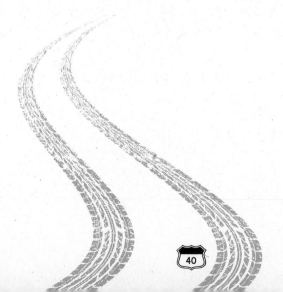

According to a May 24, 2002, article in the *Buffalo (NY) News*, a fifty-five-year-old man from Canaseraga, New York, crashed his car in a ditch while intoxicated, crawled out, and staggered onto the highway, where he was struck and killed by his intoxicated forty-three-year-old wife.

WHAT'S YOUR SIGN?

A thirty-year-old man in Kirkland, Washington, was curious to see how fast he could get his motorcycle to display on a radar sign. So he cruised to the end of the street, turned the bike around, and raced full throttle toward the sign. He watched as the radar sign registered 50 mph, and then the lights went out—because he had crashed head-on into the sign. The man was taken to the Evergreen Hospital Medical Center and treated for numerous cuts and bruises following the July 1994 incident.

DO BEE A GOOD BEE

When a tractor-trailer flipped over and spilled its contents on Interstate 435 and Interstate 35 North in Kansas City, Missouri, the events created quite a buzz in the community. That's because the truck was hauling five hundred beehives filled with approximately twenty-five million honeybees. According to a March 2008 Associated Press article, bee handlers combed the area and were able to lure most of the bees back to the hives, but several million swarmed away. The driver of the truck was uninjured but the citation he received for careless and imprudent driving will leave a stinging mark on his driving record.

"NZ Train Driver on Stress Leave after Running Over Garden Gnome"

—Reuters headline, January 20, 2004

IMPROPER LANE CHANGE

A woman driving a truck in Atlanta, Georgia, suddenly swerved across several lanes, causing twenty-four vehicles to crash and leaving eleven people with minor injuries, reported CNN in June 2003. The woman admitted she had caused the accidents but stated she was only trying to get under an overpass when it began to rain in order to keep the sofa she was hauling from getting wet.

AN UNMENTIONABLE ACCIDENT

A police spokesman in the town of Gotha, Germany, was quoted in a July 2003 Reuters article saying that a rear-end collision on Germany's notoriously speedy autobahn was a brief episode. By that he meant that the cause of the accident was a pair of underwear that had temporarily blinded the driver of a Volkswagen Passat, who then crashed into a truck in front of him. "The underpants landed on the driver's face, causing him to ram the truck ahead from behind," said the spokesman. The underwear under investigation were thrown from a van filled with unclothed men, and authorities had no idea why the men were driving naked.

CRASH-TEST DUMMIES

At an August 1993 demonstration in Cortland, New York, two hundred motorcyclists rode through town to protest the state's mandatory helmet law. During the demonstration, a tire blew out on one of the motorcycles and five demonstrators were thrown from their bikes. After being treated for head injuries, cuts, and bruises, the injured riders were cited for failure to wear helmets.

An auto mechanic from Alamo, Michigan, couldn't locate a mysterious rattle in a truck left for him to service, so he asked a friend to drive while he hung underneath the truck to locate the source of the noise. Unfortunately, his clothes got wound around the drive shaft. The knock is still around, but the mechanic isn't.

STOW AWAY WE GO!

As a ship left Vancouver, a thirty-six-year-old man from Nanaimo, British Columbia, tried to stow away—the hard way. The man positioned himself on a bridge knowing the ship would pass underneath him. He had a bungee cord firmly tied around his waist and he planned to jump down onto the ship, cut the cord, and gain a free cruise. As soon as the ship was in position, the man leapt from the bridge but didn't properly calculate the weight of his body, the distance of the fall, or the tension of the cord. Instead of gracefully stopping a few feet above the deck, the man slammed onto the ship's tennis court and then bounced back up. On his way back down he crashed into the railing of the stern and was left dangling above the water like a yo-yo. He finally splashed into the water where the crew of a passing boat rescued him. Life has its little ups and downs, but this guy had them all in one day.

Insurance Files
PART FOUR

The following are actual statements given by insurance policyholders describing automobile accidents in which they were involved.

"I saw the slow-moving sad-faced old gentleman as he bounced off the hood of my car."

"Coming home, I drove into the wrong house and collided with a tree I don't have."

"The indirect cause of this accident was a little guy in a small car with a big mouth."

"The accident happened because I had one eye on the [truck] in front, one eye on the pedestrian, and the other on the car behind."

"I started to slow down but the traffic was more stationary than I thought."

GONE WITH THE WIND

A careless forty-two-year-old German man left a briefcase on the roof of his car and drove down the highway in the western city of Bochum. The briefcase flew open and hundreds of pieces of paper littered the road—but the other motorists didn't mind. Why? Because the pieces of paper were tens of thousands of euros and the ensuing cavalcade of cash caused a traffic jam as motorists jumped out of their cars to collect the currency.

"Man Wakes Up on Subway with Steak Knife in Chest"
—Associated Press headline, January 9, 2004

TRACK MARKS

A train near Osaka, Japan, was forced to stop in its tracks because something was bugging the conductor. As the single-engine train, which was carrying only two passengers, began its way up a shadowy slope, the conductor noticed a swarm of millipedes on the tracks. As reported in an October 2003 article on UK news site Ananova. com, the creepy crawlies covered a 437-yard stretch of the track. He hit the brakes and the train slid to a halt, smashing millions of huge millipedes, some up to six centimeters long.

MISGUIDED AMERICAN

In October 2003, an unidentified American Vietnam War veteran from Toledo, Washington, was traveling on a vacation through Schwarzenbach, Germany. Unfamiliar with the town, he relied entirely on his car's navigation system. When the GPS told him to take a right turn, he turned right—right through the front doors of a supermarket. The car didn't stop until it crashed into a row of shelves.

VIOLATION

$100.00

No. 53

Month	Day	Year	City	State

Plate No.	VIN	Expiration date

Name	Location

According to an April 3, 2002, report from Channel4000.com in Minneapolis–St. Paul, Minnesota, a forty-seven-year-old female passenger was killed when the driver of the car she was in accidentally smashed into a "Welcome to Minnesota" sign on Interstate 94.

Signature	Officer No.

I'M NOT WHO I THINK I AM

A thirty-six-year-old man, referred to only as Arkadiy V., was arrested on suspicion of murder as he attempted to cross the border from Russia to Latvia. So why was he suspected of murder? Because, unfortunately, the passport he had illegally purchased belonged to an actual murder suspect still at large in Russia. The man pleaded with authorities that he wasn't a Russian citizen and that he wasn't the man on his passport. It turned out that he was telling the truth. He was charged in the October 2003 case of mistaken identity with presenting a false ID to state officials.

"Whoopee? Oopsie! Honk If the Dealership Used Your Car for Sex"

—*St. Petersburg (FL) Times* headline, February 28, 2003

A CHANGE OF PACE

A truck driver rolling his rig on U.S. 6 in La Porte, Indiana, crashed through two fences, and the impact, it seemed, must have blown him out of his clothes—because he was naked. Fifty-nine-year-old Terry Gilmore claimed the accident happened after he had set his truck's cruise control so he could change clothes, and he misjudged a curve in the road. No charges were filed in the November 2003 incident.

LIMP BLIMP

It certainly wasn't a good year for a cameraman aboard the 192-foot-long Goodyear blimp after it got away from the ground crew. The airship, *Spirit of America*, was supposed to circle around before landing after videotaping an NBA game at the Staples Center in Los Angeles, but it came loose from its moorings, bumped into a parked truck, and then crash-landed into a fertilizer pile next to a plant nursery. The cameraman suffered a knee injury in the December 2003 accident and was taken to a hospital.

CRUISING THE INTERNET

We've all heard about surefire ways of getting out of a traffic ticket, but one New Jersey man logged on to the best one—he logged in online. Sean Leach was pulled over in his 1992 Mazda 626 by North Brunswick patrolman Jason Zier, who told him his vehicle's registration had expired. Before the tow truck arrived, Leach called a friend on his cell phone, who logged on to the New Jersey Motor Vehicle Commission's online registration service and registered Leach's car. The officer still wrote Leach a ticket for the December 2003 infraction but had to cancel the tow truck, thus saving Leach the towing fee.

FLIPPING OUT

While driving in his pest-control truck, thirty-seven-year-old Jeff Goza accidentally cut off the driver of a Volvo in Gurnee, Illinois, on August 1, 2007. The driver of the Volvo, Steven Stankovitch, was enraged at Goza's perceived slight and began "aggressively" following him and finally decided to pay Goza back by cutting him off. As Stankovitch attempted this simple maneuver, he lost control of his Volvo, hit the curb, and rolled his car at least four times before coming to a stop upside down in a parking lot. Goza saw the bloodied and bruised man crawl out of the wreckage and stopped his truck to help. Stankovitch, who is five inches shorter and easily a hundred pounds lighter, shoved Goza when he realized who he was. "I wasn't going to hit him back," Goza said. Stankovitch's shoving left some blood on Goza's shirt and arms but otherwise didn't faze him. Police charged Stankovitch with reckless driving and battery and let Goza go.

HE SAID, SHE SAID

Richard Ward claimed he was ordered to get off a United Airlines flight and change clothes before he could continue with his connecting flight home to London. Ward showed United staff his British passport, but they said he wouldn't be allowed to fly until he looked more like the photo on it. What was the problem? Ward was dressed as a woman. Ward, also known as Sarah West, is a transsexual—he even had a letter from his doctor proving it. Ward filed a lawsuit against the airline in August 2001 for $50,000, and it doesn't look like they'll be able to skirt it.

Three road workers fixing guardrails in Pennsylvania were injured and taken to a local hospital after a car struck a "Men at Work" sign, which then slammed into the three men.

OH, CHUTE!

"I've never heard of anything like that before," FAA spokesman John Clabes said. "You hear about fatalities when people jump out of planes and their chutes don't open, but not this." He was talking about parachutist Michele Thibaudeau, who, while practicing a skydiving formation with twenty other jumpers in May 2001, was killed instantly when she struck the plane's propeller.

"SUV Owner Ignorant"

—*Salem (OR) Statesman Journal* headline, December 21, 2003

BETTER THAN A BRAIN BUCKET

Mechanic Gerald Marotta of El Sereno, California, was depressed after California enacted a new law in January 1992 requiring all motorcyclists to wear helmets. Marotta, who, according to his wife, always rode helmetless as a means of relaxing and dealing with problems, shot himself to death several days after the law went into effect. A portion of his suicide note read, "Now I can't even ride."

TORO!

The February 23, 1992, "Police Report" column of the *Kerrville (TX) Daily Times* described the following confrontation: A Kerrville police officer arrested a twenty-three-year-old man for assault after he allegedly tried to gore the off-duty officer with the deer antlers he had strapped to the handlebars of his bicycle.

According to an August 5, 2003, article in the *Toronto Star*, a twenty-nine-year-old man caused a traffic jam after stopping his vehicle in the passing lane on the highway because "he was too nervous to drive in the rain."

A BATHROOM BREAK

An unnamed man was denied permission to bring a cooler back aboard an American Airlines flight from New York when it was discovered he had been carrying a live ferret. The man took the ferret into an airport restroom during a layover in St. Louis and attempted to flush it down the toilet. When he realized that wouldn't work, he beat the ferret to death. When the man attempted to board the plane again, explaining that he had killed the ferret, he was arrested and couldn't weasel his way out.

"Woman Hit Twice by Same Car in 24 Hours"

—Reuters headline, March 12, 1999

PLANE LUCKY

Although he had never been in an airplane before, let alone flown one, twenty-one-year-old Louis Paul Kadlecek, in an effort to escape to Mexico after committing a crime, broke into a hangar at an airport near Lake Jackson, Texas, and stole a Cessna 172 Skyhawk. Kadlecek fiddled around with the controls until he got the engine running and then was miraculously able to get the plane off the ground. The novice navigator flew the Skyhawk for nearly a mile until crashing it into power lines and destroying the plane. Kadlecek again defied the odds by walking away from the February 29, 2004, accident unhurt. But his luck ran out the next day after eyewitnesses described him to police and he was arrested at his home.

DRIVEN TO THE LIMIT

A British woman who was driving to Calais, in northern France, to run an errand in May 2001 got lost en route. The woman claimed she couldn't find a place to turn around and eventually wound up driving five thousand miles through Europe. The unidentified woman drove through France, across the Pyrenees (the mountain range between France and Spain), across Spain, and into Gibraltar. During the extended excursion, she camped out at night with equipment that was fortunately stored in the car. She was finally rescued by her boyfriend and returned home.

Insurance Files
PART FIVE

The following are actual statements given by insurance policyholders describing automobile accidents in which they were involved.

"I pulled into a [rest area] with smoke coming from under the hood. I realized the car was on fire so [I] took my dog and smothered it with a blanket."

"On approach to the traffic lights the car in front suddenly broke."

"I was going at about 70 or 80 mph when my girlfriend on the pillion [second seat on a motorcycle] reached over and grabbed my testicles so I lost control."

"I didn't think the speed limit applied after midnight."

"I knew the dog was possessive about the car but I would not have asked her to drive it if I had thought there was any risk."

"Windshield broken. Cause unknown. Probably Voodoo."

FROZEN ASSETS

The owner of a metals analysis business was on a business trip and got drunk. Nothing too special about that. But while stumbling around in a stupor he broke a window to gain entry to a company-owned trailer in order to get out of the subzero temperatures. Unfortunately, he left the outside door open and passed out on the floor. When he woke up, the fingers and thumbs on both hands were so frostbitten they had to be amputated. The Wisconsin Supreme Court ruled that the man, because he was on a business trip, was entitled to worker's compensation. I'll drink to that.

"2 Killed When Tree Hits SUV on Road"

—Associated Press headline, December 21, 2003

TALES FROM A
TRAVEL AGENT

A woman in Little Rock, Arkansas, called a travel agent and said, "I want to book a flight to Pepsi-Cola on one of those computer planes." The agent thought for a moment and then responded; "Do you mean you want to fly to Pensacola on a commuter plane?" Without hesitating, the woman replied, "Yeah, whatever."

LOCKED OUT

The city clerk of Clinton, Arkansas, Charles Hicks, went on vacation in the summer of 1990 and purposely took with him the only set of keys to the city's file cabinets. Hicks told others in his office they would just have to wait until he returned before the files could be opened again. When asked what he planned to do about Hicks's actions, Mayor James Beaver refused to reprimand him and stated only that Hicks has always been very possessive of "his files." It wasn't reported where Hicks vacationed, but I hope it was in the Florida Keys.

MAGICAL MYSTERY TOUR

A television station in Nashville, Tennessee, WTVF, Channel 5, promoted a "Mission: Bermuda Triangle" trivia contest in May 1992. Viewers competed for a chance to win an all-expenses-paid seven-day vacation in Florida. Mysteriously, the contest was nullified and started over after hundreds of the initial entries disappeared.

A British tourist didn't think anyone would believe his fish story, so he brought his catch—a five-foot live shark—back to the hotel with him and placed it in the bathtub.

GOING NOWHERE FAST

In August 1991, Japan recorded the biggest traffic jam in the country's history. Following a typhoon that closed several main roads, an estimated fifteen thousand vehicles, stretching more than ninety-four miles, were at a virtual standstill.

VIOLATION $100.00

Month	Day	Year	City	State

Plate No.	VIN	Expiration date

Name	Location

A March 2, 2001, article in the *Albuquerque (NM) Journal* reported the case of Iris Martinez, who was found alive in her car at the bottom of the two-hundred-foot Rio Grande Gorge in Taos, New Mexico. In order for her car to go over the cliff, the twenty-four-year-old woman had to navigate around a large rock barrier that was designed to keep cars from going into the gorge.

Signature	Officer No.

MORE TALES FROM A
TRAVEL AGENT

A man who had booked a vacation in Orlando, Florida, called his travel agency and voiced a complaint. He lambasted the agent because he had expected his hotel room to have an ocean view. The agent was at a loss as to how the man could expect a view of the ocean, as Orlando is located in the middle of the state. The man wasn't buying the agent's explanation and screamed, "Don't lie to me. I looked on the map and Florida is a very thin state."

"Priest in Fatal Crash Improves"

—*Lakeland (FL) Ledger* headline, September 10, 2003

CHITTY CHITTY BANG BANG

According to a May 25, 2001, Associated Press article, nineteen-year-old Noah Berryman of Stroudsburg, Pennsylvania, was arrested for involuntary manslaughter only hours after receiving his driver's license. Berryman tried to get his car airborne on a hill three times; on his fourth attempt, the car flew sixty-three feet into the air and smashed into a tree, killing the two friends who were along for the ride.

The *Indianapolis Star* reported in July 2003 that Interstate 65 near Dayton, Indiana, was closed for nearly twelve hours after a car crashed into an eighteen-wheeler, causing at least fifteen barrels of soy sauce to spill onto the interstate. "It just smells terrible out here," said an Indiana State Police spokeswoman. "You won't be able to eat Chinese food for a long time after being out here."

ALL THE NEWS THAT'S FIT TO PRINT

According to a June 7, 2001, article in the *Milwaukee Journal Sentinel*, an unidentified thirty-nine-year-old man was killed instantly when he crashed his speeding car into a parked semi. Witnesses at the accident scene told police that moments before impact they could see that the driver of the car was reading a newspaper.

Insurance Files
PART SIX

The following are actual statements given by insurance policyholders describing automobile accidents in which they were involved.

"The car in front hit the pedestrian but he got up so I hit him again."

"A truck backed through my windshield into my wife's face."

"I had been shopping for plants all day and was on my way home. As I reached an intersection a hedge sprang up obscuring my vision and I did not see the other car."

WHAT GOES UP MUST COME DOWN

Paul Bodey, a thirty-one-year-old veteran of more than nine hundred parachute jumps, leaped from a plane at fourteen thousand feet over Sydney, Australia, and realized the worst fear of any skydiver—his chute wouldn't open. Bodey plunged a mile, crashed into a tree, and fell into the path of an oncoming car. But miraculously he wasn't killed: The tree cushioned his fall, and the driver of the car swerved in time to avoid hitting him. Bodey was taken to the hospital with a punctured lung and spinal injuries but was listed in stable condition after the March 2001 incident.

"Southwest Fires Pilots for Takeoff—Of Their Uniforms"

—*USA Today* headline, April 24, 2003

THIS IS ONLY A TEST

The following are more real answers received on exams given by the California Department of Transportation's driving school:

Q: What are some points to remember when passing or being passed?
A: Make eye contact and wave "hello" if he/she is cute.

Q: What is the difference between a flashing red traffic light and a flashing yellow traffic light?
A: The color.

Q: How do you deal with heavy traffic?
A: Heavy psychedelics.

INSURANCE RIDER

Employees of the Coachman Insurance Company in Toronto watched as the driver of a 1990 Pontiac Bonneville jumped curbs, crashed into another car, and knocked over a brick wall in the company parking lot. The driver of the car leaped out, fell to his knees, and threw his hands up as if in prayer. He yelled, "I didn't do it, honest to God I didn't do it. Someone hit me," to Cynthia Cormier, the owner of a car he had damaged. What was embarrassing about the incident is that the driver's father was inside the insurance company collecting a check for a prior accident involving the same car that had been written off and shouldn't have been on the road; the other embarrassing element was that the driver was the man's ten-year-old son. The boy wasn't charged because of his age, but his father is responsible for the eight thousand dollars in damages he caused. .

CASHING OUT ON CASHING OUT

Canadian Robert Daniel Irving was driving his twenty-two-year-old wife while intoxicated and caused an accident in which she lost her life. Irving pleaded guilty to DUI but still applied for spousal death benefits from the Manitoba Public Insurance fund. A May 10, 2002, Canadian Press article reported that the Manitoba agency reviewed Irving's claim and concluded that his guilty plea was irrelevant to his eligibility to receive benefits for his wife's death. The article also reported that he stood to be awarded the equivalent of $28,500 U.S. dollars in death benefits.

"Carelessness Cited as Cause of Accident"

—Associated Press headline, February 24, 2007

AN IDEA THAT WENT BUST

James Suchomski, twenty-five, of Tampa, Florida, and his friend Josh Edleman, twenty-six, filled nearly a dozen small balloons with explosive acetylene gas with the intention of setting them off to celebrate Independence Day 2002. The men put all the balloons in Suchomski's car and jumped in, and the next thing they knew they were lying on the ground outside the car. The car "looked like a sardine can," said a Tampa Police bomb technician. "It was as if you just took the roof and peeled it off." Apparently a spark from either the ignition or from slamming the car door had caused the balloons to explode, destroying the car and leaving the men with burns, bruises, and hearing damage.

SHOPPING À LA CARTE

Police responded to a call from a grocery store in Wood River, Illinois, complaining about a man stealing one of their grocery carts. But this wasn't any normal wobbly wheeled manual grocery cart; this was a $2,500 motorized marvel. Witnesses told officers they saw a man, Harold P. Bennett, drive off with the cart filled with groceries (which he had purchased), turn down a highway, and stop at an apartment complex. According to a July 2002 article in the *St. Louis Post-Dispatch*, the forty-one-year-old man was arrested for theft; since he was drunk and the cart was a motorized vehicle, he was also charged with driving under the influence.

USE CAUTION WHILE OPERATING ANY VEHICLE

A police officer in Bethlehem, Pennsylvania, spotted thirty-year-old John Powell slowly driving down the street, so he sounded his siren and showed his badge, but the man didn't pull over. Finally, the officer got out of his patrol car and walked up to the perpetrator during possibly the slowest police chase on record—with top speeds barely reaching 3 miles per hour. According to police records, Powell was riding a child's battery-operated Fisher-Price Power Wheels car; although he wasn't exceeding the speed limit, he was exceeding the vehicle's age requirement by ten times. Powell, who smelled of alcohol, said he was trying to get to his uncle's house but never said why he was driving a child's toy. A woman in the neighborhood who had called in to report her son's toy car missing decided not to press charges, but police charged Powell with public drunkenness for the August 12, 2002, incident.

A REAL CHILLY WILLY

"There's a man hanging from the top of the car . . . naked!" said Debbie DeMarco about the blue Volkswagen Jetta that drove by her on the morning of December 2, 2002. "All this guy had on was white socks and a T-shirt." According to court papers, the naked man, Michael Becker, who was as blue as the Jetta, was trying to stop his wife, Lori Ann, from taking the family car and had jumped on the hood in his birthday clothes in the seventeen-degree weather. After Lori Ann crashed the car into a concrete barrier, an "extremely cold" Michael pushed her back into the vehicle and punctured her thigh seventeen times with a small tool that was hanging from the rearview mirror. Lori Ann Becker was charged with a number of violations, including attempted homicide; Michael was cited with lesser charges.

SLOW CHILDREN AHEAD

The Disabled Student Program and Services Office of Valley College in Los Angeles, California, set a campus speed limit of 4 miles per hour, with penalties for violators ranging from a simple warning to expulsion. So was the policy put in place to stop skateboarders from half-piping into other students? Nope. According to a December 14, 2002, article in the *Los Angeles Times*, it was enacted for students in wheelchairs. Had there been a rash of accidents between wheelchair-bound students and pedestrians? Nope. "It's a safety issue," said the vice president of administration, Tom Jacobsmeyer. "A speeding wheelchair can be just as dangerous as a speeding car."

"Bathtub Lands on Highway in Bradley County"

—*Chattanoogan (TN)* headline, April 2, 2003

WHEN PIGS FLY

A South African Airways plane en route home was forced to return to Heathrow Airport in London in April 1995 after alarms alerted pilots of a potential fire. It was soon discovered that the heat and flatulence produced by the seventy-two prize stud pigs in the cargo bay had triggered the alarms.

On July 5, 2003, the BBC reported on twenty-six-year-old Becky Nyang, who was vacationing on the Greek island of Corfu when she was struck by lightning. The airport worker from Reading, Berkshire, in England, was left with severe blisters about the mouth, face, and feet (where the lightning exited) after the metal stud in her tongue attracted the lightning.

SNAKES ON A PLANE

Continental Airlines settled with the parents of five-year-old Alexandra Taylor for an undisclosed sum because the pet of another passenger had terrified the little girl during a flight in 1994, causing her to have reoccurring nightmares. Continental had allowed a female passenger to bring aboard a six-foot-long python that served as a "support snake" to help the woman overcome her fear of flying.

THOSE MAGNIFICENT MEN IN THEIR FLYING MACHINES

Reuters reported in August 1996 on fifty-one-year-old Brian Howson of Perth, Western Australia, and his remarkable plane maintenance skills. Howson repaired the landing gear on his single-engine plane at an altitude of four thousand feet by hanging out of the door, upside down, while three of his passengers held his legs.

WRONG MAN FOR THE JOB

During a May 1996 Danish Maersk Air flight from Birmingham, West Midlands, in England, to Milan, Italy, with forty-nine passengers aboard, an unidentified copilot suffered an anxiety attack. The man later resigned his position and admitted he has acrophobia—an extreme or irrational fear of heights.

VIOLATION

$100.00

No. 95

Month	Day	Year	City	State

Plate No.	VIN	Expiration date

Name	Location

"I just spent a lot of money getting my brakes repaired and I didn't want to wear them down."

—Excuse given for speeding to an Andersonville, Illinois, police officer

Signature	Officer No.

HALF-AND-HALF

"The rear half of the car was cut right off and stayed under the pole," a police spokesman from Blacktown, New South Wales, in Australia, said. "And the front portion skidded and jumped for another twenty-two meters (seventy-two feet) before it stopped with the driver still in it." Rescue crews called to the scene of the January 2003 accident found the driver, strapped in his seatbelt, virtually unharmed and still arguing with his girlfriend on his cell phone. According to an article in the *Surry Hills Daily Telegraph*, the seventeen-year-old driver was having an argument with his girlfriend when he hit a pole going approximately 94 miles per hour.

NOW I'M GOING TO GO TO DISNEY WORLD

Roy Dennis of Hampshire, a county on the south coast of England, was visiting his son Edward in Auckland, New Zealand, in October 2002 on what he had anticipated as being a vacation of a lifetime. He'll definitely remember it for a lifetime because he wound up in the hospital three times in two days. First, Dennis had to undergo emergency surgery after he snapped an ankle while skydiving and was confined to a wheelchair. Then he was bitten by a puffer fish, the most poisonous animal in the world next to the golden poison frog, and needed a tetanus shot. The next day, Dennis went to an adventure park where staff put the sixty-year-old man in his wheelchair in a special car for the tour. But the chair wasn't secured and Dennis spun out of the car and into a window, breaking his nose.

LOW RIDER

The *Sydney Morning Herald* reported on a family of three who were injured in a car crash because the mother was too drunk to drive. But she didn't really cause the accident, because although she was behind the wheel she let someone else steer—her five-year-old son. The car careened off Bli Bli Road on the Sunshine Coast, hit a tree, hurtled down an embankment, and came to rest in an enclosed field. No one in the car was wearing seatbelts. All were thrown from the car and suffered minor injuries after the January 2008 accident.

Scott Browning of Houston, Texas, was assigned an exotic dancer to be his "designated caddy" and chauffeur of his golf cart during a tournament at the Men's Club in Houston. The dancer became drunk during the event and accidentally dumped the cart into a drainage ditch, rupturing Browning's Achilles tendon. He was awarded $16,500 in damages.

IDIOT, THY NAME IS VANITY

According to a November 26, 2000, Associated Press article, Wesley Ridgwell was confronted with 705 photographs showing him speeding through tollbooths without paying. The automatic cameras took clear photographs of his late-model Honda running tollbooths from August 1999 to June 2000. Ridgwell was easy to locate because his vanity license plate reads "JST CRZY."

THERE'S SNOW PLACE LIKE HOME

A man from the Gambia, in western Africa, who was traveling on business in Germany during winter, alerted authorities that someone had painted his car white while he was asleep. Police in the town of Hildesheim discovered that the man, who had never seen snow before, thought someone had vandalized his car after finding it covered in the white stuff.

Flight crews and passengers restrained Richard Reid, who attempted to blow up American Airlines Flight 63 on December 22, 2001, with a homemade shoe bomb, and strapped him into his seat. It was reported in a June 8, 2002, Associated Press article that the explosive shoes were simply stored in the cockpit for safekeeping.

JUST HANGING OUT

Eighteen-year-old Joe Thompson was thrown more than twenty feet into the air as the result of a car crash near Highway 40 and Woods Chapel Road in Blue Springs, Missouri, in January 2003. Instead of plunging to his death, Thompson was able to "hang in there" by holding on to live overhead power lines. He was even able to use his cell phone to call his family and rescue workers—who arrived twenty minutes later and helped Thompson down. According to the January 28, 2003, article in the *Independence (MO) Examiner*, Thompson survived because the power lines were insulated.

SOCCER OR SOCK HIM

According to an April 7, 2003, article in New Zealand's *Southland Times*, during a bus ride home from a game and for reasons unknown, an Australian rugby team doffed their clothes and ran naked across the Kawarau Bridge. While on the bridge, one player saw a car approaching and decided to stick his naked butt toward it—and apparently his shiny hiney attracted the driver's attention. The car smashed into the nude dude, who wound up in a hospital with pelvis and hip injuries.

"Brighton Man Dies after Driving Vehicle into Burning House"

—*Belleville (Ontario, Canada) Intelligencer* headline, March 27, 2003

WHAT HAPPENS IN VEGAS . . .

On the night before leaving from his vacation in Las Vegas, twenty-one-year-old James Cripps, in a drunken stupor, married a complete stranger from Australia. "If you go to Las Vegas, you drink, you gamble, and you get married," Cripps said. "Which is what I did." The *Times* of London reported in November 2001 that Cripps admitted he was "too drunk to consummate" the marriage, but the worst part was telling his girlfriend back home in Bristol, England. Cripps said Abi Harding, his girlfriend, "dumped him," though the "exact nature of [her] reaction goes unrecorded."

ID AND IQ

A family of four arrived at the Baltimore-Washington International Airport all packed and ready to begin their vacation in Las Vegas. The mother, father, and son presented driver's licenses to the American Airlines ticketing agent, and the daughter presented a student ID from the University of Maryland. The clerk, however, refused to accept the daughter's card, claiming that even though the ID was issued by a state university, it didn't meet the newly enacted requirement of being "issued by a government." Without putting up a fight, the entire family abandoned their vacation plans and drove home. Incidentally, this situation happened in July 1996, long before the even stricter post-9/11 regulations.

A harried passenger called his travel agent from the airport with an urgent question: "How do I know which plane to get on?" The agent asked exactly what he meant, to which the man replied, "I was told my flight number is 823, but none of these darn planes have numbers on them."

THAT REALLY GETS MY GOAT

Taking "My dog ate my homework" to a whole new level, in August 1997, the Caron family of Sandown, New Hampshire, were granted an extension to file their quarterly tax return by the Internal Revenue Service. The Caron family reported that they would have to reconstruct their entire income tax paperwork because, while they were on vacation, their pet pygmy goats had eaten all the documentation. In addition to the tax forms, the goats also ate toilet bowl cleaner, a telephone directory, and a lampshade.

"Road Rage Rubbed Out by Massage Service"
—Associated Press headline, February 27, 2003

YOU SAY TOMATO, AND I SAY TOMATO

Raeoul Sebastian and Emma Nunn, both nineteen, of London purchased airline tickets to Sydney for a three-week vacation, and they got just what they asked for. They were planning on staying in Sydney, Australia, but they actually wound up in Sydney, Nova Scotia, in August 2002. The couple didn't realize they were headed in the wrong direction until they had a plane changeover in Halifax, Nova Scotia, after a six-hour flight from England. The confused couple decided to stay in Sydney, Nova Scotia, for a few days and then save their money for a real trip to Sydney, Australia, the following year.

A REAL RAT RACE

"You can just imagine a nice, sunny day on Cleveleys Prom, eating your chips, and then this thing goes whizzing past," said a Cleveleys, Lancashire, police officer in England. He was referring to complaints by vacationers that they were forced to run for cover when they saw a hamster in a race car barreling down the promenade. The hamster, nicknamed Speedy, was apprehended in a toy racing car, powered by a hamster wheel in the middle, and handed over to an animal sanctuary.

A twenty-three-year-old Belgian woman, traveling by ferry from Greece to Italy, was detained in Brindisi, Italy, in July 2002 for trying to smuggle her boyfriend in a large suitcase.

A DEAD-END STREET

Eighty-two-year-old Shulamit Dezhin finally passed her driver's test in Ashdod, Israel, in March 1997, after thirty-five failed attempts. Dezhin said she was motivated to pass her driving test because she wanted to drive to Tel Aviv to visit her parents. Unfortunately, it took her so long to obtain her license that both her parents were dead by the time it was finally issued.

A PORTION OF JUSTICE

- Gourmet Howard Schaeffer convinced a New York City jury in March 1991 that he no longer had his invaluable senses of taste and smell as a result of a traffic accident. When questioned as to why, if that were true, he still weighed more than two hundred pounds, Schaeffer claimed he discovered alternative ways of enjoying food: "It's amazing how quickly you can get into texture." The jury swallowed his reasoning and awarded him $1.1 million.

"Collapsed Bridge in China Faulty"

—Associated Press headline, November 11, 1999

PLANE REASONING

Wim Kodman, one of the 280 passengers out of 340 who survived the crash of a Dutch charter plane in Faro, Portugal, told reporters in December 1993 how he had tried to calm a friend shortly before impact. Kodman, who is a botanist, recalled, "I told him, 'I'm a scientist; we're objective.' I told him a crash was improbable. I was trying to remember the exact probability when we smashed into the ground."

A forty-three-year-old man from Richmond, Virginia, was hospitalized after being blown off the top of a van traveling 50 miles per hour. Authorities said the man had been lying on top of the van holding down a bundle of wooden fencing when a gust of wind blew him off.

FLY THE FRIENDLY SKIES

During a flight from Berlin to Tel Aviv in August 1991, an unidentified woman in her forties jumped into the aisle, tore off her dress, and shouted, "Bring me Shamir. I want Shamir," referring to Yitzhak Shamir, then the Israeli prime minister. As she was being led off the plane with her only piece of luggage, a plastic bag containing about thirty thousand dollars in cash, the woman bit one of the crew members.

RETURN TO SENDER

In September 2003, twenty-five-year-old Charles D. McKinley of Brooklyn, New York, decided to take all four weeks of his earned vacation and visit his parents in DeSoto, Texas. Soon the shipping clerk was all packed for his vacation—and when I say he was packed, I mean just that. He packed himself in a shipping crate, had himself air-expressed to his parents' house, and charged everything to his employer. When McKinley arrived on his parents' doorstep he broke through the box, shook hands with the "shaken and frightened" deliveryman, and went in to surprise his folks. The driver called the police, and soon the FBI, the FAA, the U.S. attorney's office, postal inspectors, and the Transportation Security Administration wrapped up McKinley in a case of their own. According to the *Dallas Morning News*, McKinley was charged as a stowaway, which is a federal misdemeanor.

THE RETURN FLIGHT
OF THE LIVING DEAD

Scott Bender boarded a U.S. Airways flight from North Carolina to Birmingham, Alabama, and did what a lot of passengers do—he fell asleep. However, when this jewelry salesman woke up, he "didn't know if he was alive or dead," said Bender's lawyer. That's because the plane had already landed, all the passengers and crew were gone, the lights were off, and the plane was parked. So Bender came to the most logical conclusion—he was dead. The *Birmingham News* reported on October 4, 2001, that Bender sued U.S. Airways for negligence, stating that he suffered mental and emotional anguish because of the terrifying event.

LETTING MORE THAN A CAT OUT OF THE BAG

James and Jane McDonald were surprised to find that a brown bag filled with ashes had smashed through the backyard deck of their home in Grand Forks, North Dakota, on December 29, 2001. They contacted the authorities and, according to the *Grand Forks Herald*, a local environmental health official listed the most likely explanation was that someone had thrown the bag from an airplane. Further investigation showed that the ashes were cremated human remains that a loved one must have been scattering when he or she accidentally dropped the bag.

According to a July 11, 2002, article in London's *Daily Telegraph*, a seventeen-year-old woman who had just arrived in England from Dubai was detained when airport agents noticed that the faux chameleon pattern on her hat was, in fact, an endangered—and very much alive—real chameleon.

FLY UNITED

Pilot Thomas Hayashi welcomed a couple in their fifties aboard his charter plane for a grown-up version of "Seven Minutes in Heaven." The couple had booked the flight advertising "Mile-High Club" tours, and soon the plane was some forty miles south of Key West, Florida. Suddenly the "friendly skies" took an unfriendly turn when the couple attacked Hayashi with a knife and ordered him to take them to Cuba. Hayashi banked sharply, trying to throw the armed hijackers off balance, and during the ensuing fracas the plane crashed into the sea. According to an August 2001 article in the *Miami Herald*, Hayashi survived the crash but the couple did not.

BY THE SEAT OF HIS CARGO PANTS

Stowaways on planes are a very uncommon occurrence, and stories of people who accidentally become stowaways are even less common—but they do still happen. According to Norman Black, a United Parcel Service spokesman in Atlanta, Georgia, a cargo loader at an Anchorage, Alaska, airport took an unscheduled nap during a work break and wound up headed for China. "It wasn't like he was ten minutes away and the pilot could just turn around," Black said. "The plane was out over the Pacific Ocean, well on its way to Hong Kong." The man fell asleep in the cargo hold of a Boeing 747, and I'm sure by the time the stewardess got there with the serving cart all the good meals had been taken.

THEY CAN'T TAKE A JOKE

A passenger boarding an America West Airlines flight in July 2002 made an offhand remark to a flight attendant and was soon handed off to authorities. The woman's remark was about a previous incident involving an America West Airlines pilot and copilot who were arrested for trying to fly an airliner drunk. She asked the attendant if they had "checked the crew for sobriety." A spokeswoman for the airlines, Patty Nowack, defended the decision to throw the woman off the flight, saying, "Safety is no joking matter." Nowack explained that, "While this passenger may have been joking, it is difficult to determine if someone is joking or serious. We take any comment regarding safety seriously."

ALL THERE IN BLACK AND WHITE

Hoping the people at the Department of Motor Vehicles in Hicksville, New York, were color-blind, Ronald Sturkes allegedly arranged for a fifty-five-year-old black man to take his place on the written test. Sturkes, who is twenty-seven years old and white, was already well-known to the employees of the DMV after his explosive protests stemming from his failure in the driving portion of the test. He was charged with irregularities in taking his driver's license test.

VIOLATION $100.00

Month	Day	Year	City	State

Plate No.		VIN		Expiration date

Name		Location	

A man on a water scooter on Lake Michigan was missing for two days when Coast Guard personnel finally located him sitting on his scooter and suffering from sunstroke and dehydration. The man hadn't had any water for two days, which confused the Coast Guard because Lake Michigan is a freshwater lake.

Signature	Officer No.

THE ROAD TO PERDITION

The Chicago Apostolic Assembly Church youth group set off for what they hoped would be a spiritual excursion to California over the 1994 Thanksgiving holiday. But the trip quickly turned from "Onward Christian Soldiers" to "Highway to Hell." Various complications delayed their exodus from Chicago for two days, and then their bus endured numerous breakdowns, including a tire blowout in Missouri. The group was forced to partake of a Thanksgiving meal consisting entirely of junk food instead of the traditional meal planned for them in California. Their bus had clutch failure while in the mountains of Arizona during a blizzard, and they were forced to spend two days in a cramped hotel in Flagstaff awaiting repairs. The emergency cash they requested never arrived; the bathrooms were unsanitary; and the driver, who was diabetic, had convulsions while behind the wheel. The New Mexico police finally ended their misery after issuing citations because the bus was considered an unsafe vehicle.

TRACK MARKS

Michael Runyon of Kewanee, Illinois, was arrested for drunken driving in the summer of 1991 after he literally tried to mow down an oncoming freight train. Runyon, whose driver's license was suspended in 1986, had been using his five-horsepower riding lawnmower as transportation ever since, and he accidentally drove the mower onto the tracks of an oncoming train. Amazingly, Runyon was unhurt after the train smashed into him and flung his mower ten feet into the air, which gives new meaning to the phrase "cutting it close."

"Crashed Jet May Have Flown Too Low"

—Associated Press headline, April 24, 2000

THE THIRD TIME WAS A CHARM

"I like to think of them as landings because I walked away," said thirty-one-year-old pilot Justin Kirkbride of Farmington, New Mexico, of his two crashes in one day, January 10, 2002. The first happened when Kirkbride had mechanical problems with his single-engine Cessna 172 Skyhawk and crash-landed in a patch of trees in the mountains of Colorado. He left his two passengers and walked six hours in knee-deep snow until he got to a ridge where his cell phone worked so he could call for help. As Kirkbride knew the exact location of the stranded passengers, he boarded one of two MH-53J Pave Low helicopters from Kirtland Air Force Base in Albuquerque, New Mexico, and set off to rescue them. Once at the crash scene, the helicopter in which Kirkbride was riding went into a spin and crashed near the Cessna. No one was hurt in the second accident, but the victims of the first crash were taken to the hospital for serious but non-life-threatening injuries.

THE ROAD LESS TRAVELED

Pilot David Nickerson was three sheets to the wind when he mistook a Maryland road for a runway, landed his plane, realized his mistake, and then asked bystanders to stop traffic so he could take off again. Before you could say "contact," someone contacted the police, who found three open whiskey bottles in his plane. Since Nickerson landed on a highway on that January 2001 day, he was charged with possession of an open container and negligent driving. If, however, he had landed at a general aviation airport, he would have gotten off scot-free because there are no regulations in place to check the sobriety of private pilots.

A Chinese man was arrested when the flight he was on landed in Shanghai. According to a July 1, 2002, article in the *Strait-Times* of Singapore, the man, who had never flown before, had attempted to open the emergency exit door while in flight because he wanted to spit.

YOU'RE IN REALLY GOOD HANDS . . .

According to a February 4, 1994, article in the *Daily Oklahoman*, several motorists were uncovered by the Oklahoma City police having purchased automobile liability insurance under "God's Insurance Policy." The heavenly insured were convinced by a salesman that the policy (mainly filled with biblical scripture) would fulfill the requirements of Oklahoma's mandatory-insurance law. The $285 policy claimed that "fear" was the primary cause of accidents and since the policy was "issued by the Father, Son and the Holy Ghost," it would protect the policyholder better than conventional insurance would.

A driving instructor from Parkersburg, West Virginia, was allowed to keep his job as a driving instructor at the local high school—even after he was arrested for drunken driving.

A FRENCH SNOB

Michel Thibodeau, a thirty-four-year-old computer technician with the Canadian House of Commons, sued Air Canada for more than $500,000 because he could not order a 7UP in French. During a flight from Montreal to Ottawa on August 14, 2000, Thibodeau boarded the plane with a friendly *"bonjour,"* and the flight attendant answered in English. More frustrating to Thibodeau was when he tried to order a 7UP in French and was served a Sprite instead.

In December 2007, Thibodeau was in the news once again after filing an official complaint against Ottawa's OC Transpo, the city's public transit company, demanding bus drivers greet riders with *"bonjour"* as well as "hello."

THE BEST OF THE WORST

In February 1997, forty-five-year-old Sue Evans-Jones of Yate, Gloucestershire, in England, passed her driver's test after three failed attempts. However, Evans-Jones drove away ten instructors during the 1,800 lessons and twenty-seven years she took to learn her driving skills. Most of the instructors had told her she was such a terrible driver that it would be best if she never received a license.

"Woman Dies in Crash Caused by Monkey"

—*Star* (Malaysia) headline, February 13, 2003

FRONT-END COLLISION

Charmaine Johnston suffered brain damage and was partially paralyzed in a car accident in 1985. She sued the driver of the car that had struck her and in February 1994 a judge in Sydney, Australia, awarded her $1.5 million. As part of the settlement, a portion of the money was designated to care for Johnson's two-year-old son. But why was money allocated for a child born seven years after the accident? Because, the judge ruled, Johnson's brain damage caused her to act "impulsively and without judgment or thought of consequences" when approached to have sex, which led to her pregnancy.

A SIDE ORDER OF JUSTICE

During her four-day trial, forty-eight-year-old Sarah Milliken attempted to prove that she suffered chronic back injuries as a result of her car skidding out of control on an icy spot in the road and that the Pennsylvania Department of Transportation should be held responsible. She ultimately lost her March 1996 case in Greensburg, Pennsylvania, after her husband supplied the court with a videotape of Milliken dressed in a bathing suit and wrestling with another woman in a vat of coleslaw during Biker Week in Daytona Beach, Florida.

"Snake Found in Hawaii-Bound Passenger's Pants"

—Associated Press headline, February 6, 2003

IT'S HAMER TIME

Howard Hamer had just taken off in his home-built single-engine Lancer 236 airplane from Chiloquin, Oregon, when the engine suddenly lost all power. The sixty-three-year-old pilot decided to attempt an emergency landing northbound on U.S. 97 when an empty logging flatbed truck driven by Filiberto Corona Ambriz pulled up underneath him. According to an August 12, 2000, article in the *Minneapolis (MN) Star Tribune*, "The plane's propeller snagged on the sleeper of the truck, and the tail crashed down onto the empty flatbed trailer." No one was hurt in the accident, but authorities believe that serious injuries would have occurred if Hamer had landed on the highway.

OVER AND UNDER

According to a Reuters article from January 28, 2002, an overweight man who fell asleep on a passenger train heading to Manchester, England, slid out of his seat, became wedged under a table—and couldn't get out. Firefighters struggled for forty-five minutes before finally freeing the portly passenger.

The *Age*, a newspaper in Melbourne, Victoria, in Australia, reported a story on June 19, 2003, about a Chinese man who wanted to start a scorpion farm and was transporting six hundred scorpions in a simple cardboard box on a commuter train. According to terrified eyewitness accounts, during the ride all six hundred of the arachnids crawled out of the box and scampered throughout the train.

STONE-COLD SUSPECT

A tourist traveling by train through Skegness, Lincolnshire, in England, in July 2001 thought she had spotted a real local attraction and called police to complain about a dancing naked man with long hair and a beard. It didn't take authorities long to realize that the woman was talking about a statue of the town's mascot, the "Jolly Fisherman." Inspector Paul Elliot reported that some of his men were "amused" at the mistaken identity but that the "woman made the call in good faith and we responded as we always do." I guess that means this had happened before.

Insurance Files
PART SEVEN

The following are actual statements given by insurance policyholders describing automobile accidents in which they were involved.

"I was sure the old fellow would never make it to the other side of the road when I struck him."

"The pedestrian had no idea which way to run as I ran over him."

"I had been learning to drive with power steering. I turned the wheel to what I thought was enough and found myself in a different direction going the opposite way."

URINE BAD SHAPE

A Frankfurt, Germany, court ordered Deutsche Bahn (German Railway) to pay a man $270 in compensation for what they called his "torture." Apparently the man was on a two-hour train ride in April 2002 that had no working toilets—they had all been locked because there was no water for flushing.

"KLM Plane Filled with Excrement"

—Reuters headline, January 23, 2003

A SLAP ON THE WRIST AND A THUMP ON THE HEAD

According to an October 6, 2001, *Queensland [Australia] Courier-Mail* article, Supreme Court Justice Peter McClellan ruled against Kane Rundle's claim for more than one million dollars in compensation for brain damage suffered when his head collided with a support pole as he leaned out of a train to spray-paint graffiti on a wall. Rundle argued that the State Rail Authority was negligent "because it had failed to ensure a carriage window could not be opened far enough to put his body through."

IN THE ROUGH

Diana J. Nagy filed a lawsuit in 1996 in Charleston, West Virginia, following a fatal drinking and driving accident in which her husband and son were involved. Nagy didn't sue the driver of the other car, because there was no other driver—in fact, there was no car. Mr. Nagy had been drinking at a golf tournament at the Berry Hills Country Club when he fell out of the golf cart and died. Mrs. Nagy sued both the manufacturer of the golf cart (that she claimed should have come with seatbelts) and her son, who was driving the cart.

"Driver Shocked as Sheep Emerges from Pothole"

—*Western Mail*, Wales, September 23, 2000

THE SKIN OF YOUR TEETH

According to Canadian police reports from February 1995, a family in Edmonton, Alberta, was involved in an accident when the driver temporarily lost consciousness, collided with another car, and then smashed into a utility pole. The occupants of both cars survived relatively unscathed. The father, who was driving the car, was listening to his twenty-two-year-old son, who had had oral surgery earlier in the day, describe in gory detail the extraction of his wisdom teeth when he became woozy and passed out.

The *Independent* of London reported on September 30, 2003, about the cause of a delay in the Tube train in London's Underground. Apparently a trainee driver had pleaded with two colleagues to stop discussing the grisly details of a recent vasectomy operation. When they continued with their conversation, the trainee passed out and fell out of the cab.

SEEING DOUBLE

Donna Endicott was cruising down Interstate 84 near Portland, Oregon, in May 1991 when she noticed that the car ahead of her was, in fact, hers—it had been stolen earlier. Endicott tailed the stolen car for nearly a half hour and watched as it stopped in front of a house and the two thieves got out. She immediately jumped out of her new car and got into her old car and drove away. When the thieves left the house they had just burglarized, they had no getaway car. In less than an hour, they were riding in another car—a police car.

"Man Smuggled Monkeys in Pants"

—Reuters headline, December 20, 2003

A BRIEF ENCOUNTER

A German man hid in the bathroom on a train in June 2002 in order to avoid paying for a ticket. When the train stopped in Hanau, Germany, he jumped off and tried to get away, but the police gave chase and soon had him under arrest. Once the man was at the police station, he pulled off his pants and ripped off his underwear and then began hitting one of the officers in the face with it. He was charged with causing bodily harm and obstructing police.

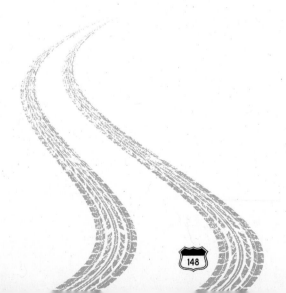

BOYS AND THEIR TOYS

When Carol Dukes discovered that her eleven-year-old son, Charlie, had left his Game Boy behind when he went to camp she decided to take it to him. She left her home in Berkshire, England, in September 2001 and traveled by plane, taxis, and a ferry to find him on the isolated island of Iona, Scotland. "If you decide to do something you do it and worry about the money later," Dukes said. "But I think everyone was quite surprised to see me." They weren't so surprised to see Dukes, but they were surprised to see the Game Boy; Charlie was attending camp "to learn about life without modern amenities."

Earl Teichmann, a thirty-six-year-old Australian cyclist, had to undergo extensive facial reconstruction after a kangaroo ricocheted off a car and struck him.

JACK FROST NIPPED AT MORE THAN HIS NOSE

Britain's heat wave in August 2003 claimed dozens of sunburn and heat exhaustion victims, but one man, traveling from London to Manchester, suffered a case of frostbite. "It was incredibly hot," Mike Ball, forty-six, told the *Guardian* newspaper. "I slipped off my shoe and sock because my car is an automatic and I don't need to use my left foot." Ball kept his toes too close to the air-conditioning vent on the 248-mile journey and was treated for mild frostbite.

A DOG'S LIFE

"I've been in firefighting for many years, but I've never seen anything like this happen," Fire Chief Gary Gilliam of Culdesac, Idaho, said. According to an October 6, 2003, Associated Press article, a man's car backfired, igniting the fur on his dog. The dog ran into a field, rolled around to put out the flames, and accidentally started a grass fire off U.S. Highway 95. Firefighters quickly put out the flames and reported that the dog was unhurt but did smell of burned hair. Wow, a double whammy—wet dog and burned hair smell.

"Speeding Motorist Blamed Coke"

—Associated Press headline, December 13, 2002

EWWWWWWW!!!!

Truck driver Ricky Walter of Waukesha, Wisconsin, crashed into another vehicle in October 1997 and was trapped inside the cab. The force of the impact filled Walter's cab with the contents of the load he was carrying, and he was stuck inside for more than half an hour. Unfortunately, Walter was driving a sewage truck at the time.

A June 12, 2004, Associated Press article reported the tragic story of Jeff Frolio, a cameraman for Omaha, Nebraska, television station KETV, who, while shooting a story about a dangerous intersection in West Omaha, walked out into the intersection and was struck and killed by an oncoming car.

SIGNING OFF

In September 1995, thirty-one-year-old Robert Kevin Brown died in a single-car accident on Interstate 95 in Prince William County, Virginia, after his truck plummeted into a ravine. According to the Virginia State Police, Brown was apparently unhappy because the flow of traffic was traveling at only 55 miles per hour. Eyewitnesses claimed that Brown leaned out of his truck window to make a rude gesture to another driver, lost control of his vehicle, and plunged into the ravine.

"German Driver Beaten for Observing Speed Limit"

—Reuters headline, July 30, 2004

SHALLOW PEOPLE— DEEP POCKETS

Mary Ubaudi of Madison County, Illinois, was a passenger in a car driven by William Humphrey. She claimed that he was going too fast, lost control of the car in a construction zone, and flipped the car, throwing her from the vehicle and causing her to sustain severe and life-threatening injuries. So Ubaudi sued Humphrey—no big deal, right? Well, it wouldn't be interesting enough for this book except that Ubaudi didn't just sue Humphrey for "at least $50,000"; she also sued Rowe Construction for "at least $50,000" and Mazda Motors, the manufacturer of Humphrey's Miata, for "in excess of $150,000." According to a November 2004 article in the *Madison County Record*, Ubaudi's lawsuit claimed the car manufacturer "failed to provide instructions regarding the safe and proper use of a seatbelt."

DAY TRIPPER

It was no joke, but it did happen on April Fool's Day in 2000. That's when Philadelphia, Pennsylvania, police officer Margo Grady, escorting a rape victim from one stationhouse to another one only three miles away, took a wrong turn and wound up on the New Jersey Turnpike. Grady had traveled almost to Newark, seventy-five miles away, before she turned on her blue lights, pulled over a car, and asked the driver where she was.

"Dead Driver Given Fine"

—News.com.au headline, August 11, 2003

GIVE ME A BRAKE!

John Clayton III was sitting in the backseat of a car when the driver suddenly slammed on the brakes, causing, he claimed, "back problems." A jury in Greensboro, North Carolina, agreed with Clayton and awarded him $1.5 million, according to a September 28, 2003, article in the *Charlotte Observer*. So what's the big deal? Clayton, at the time of the accident, was being taken to the police station on an outstanding warrant and was riding in the backseat of a police cruiser when the arresting officer slammed on the brakes.

THE FOLLICLE FOLLIES

A British motorist was cruising down the M6 motorway letting his long hair flap in the breeze when it started to rain. He pressed the button to close the electric sunroof and immediately had a hair-raising experience—his hair was caught and he was being pulled out of the driver's seat. The bad news is that the man was yanked away from the steering wheel and lost control of the car, which was careening down the motorway at 70 miles per hour. The good news is that the man was also pulled away from the accelerator, and the car eventually drifted to a stop in the middle of the motorway.

"AAA Says Record Gas Price Predictions May or May Not Come True"

—*Kingsport (TN) Times-News* headline, July 11, 2006

THAT MOTOR'S PURRING LIKE A KITTEN

Late for her massage therapy class, Torri Hutchinson found herself speeding down the freeway near Blackfoot, Idaho, steering with one hand and putting on lipstick with the other when she noticed a man in the car next to her frantically signaling her to pull over. Hutchinson, thinking the man was a police officer, pulled over, and the man bolted out of his car and pulled Hutchinson's terrified cat from the ski rack on top of her car's roof. Hutchinson told reporters for the *Idaho State Journal* in March 2005 that she didn't realize the cat was there and that she had even stopped for gas ten miles earlier without noticing it. "She's always on my car," Hutchinson admits. And to quell anyone's negative judgment of her, she remarked to the reporter, "I'm not an airhead." No word as to the color of Ms. Hutchinson's hair.

TAKING POSSESSION OF HER CAR

This story is very similar to Steven King's novel *Christine*, about a creepy 1958 Plymouth Fury that kills people, but in this case the owner's name, not the car's, is Christine. After Christine Djordjevic's car seemingly started up and crashed into her neighbor's house by itself she knew it was "possessed." According to an April 2005 article in the *Northwest Indiana Times*, police investigating the crime were skeptical about Djordjevic's claim until they saw it for themselves. It turns out that the car has a remote starter and if Djordjevic left the car in gear and pushed the button on her key fob, the car would take off. Even though the car had done the same thing several times, including lurching away with her son inside, Djordjevic never did anything about it. "I don't even know how the stupid thing works," she says. "It usually does it by accident."

BANGERS AND MASH

John Hatfield, forty-six, was driving near his home in South Woodham Ferrers, in the borough of Chelmsford in Essex, England, on a warm day with his window down when something flew in and hit him squarely on the nose. "He lost quite a lot of blood from his injury," said paramedic Dave Holton, who was called to the scene. "After we cleaned him he decided not to go to hospital but he has been left with a very swollen nose." According to an April 20, 2005, article in the *Guardian*, Hatfield was struck on the face with a sausage. The sausage tosser remains on the loose and police said they are handling the case as an assault. Since the guy's name is Hatfield I wonder if they suspect a McCoy. Throwing sausage at someone is rash but throwing bacon would have been rasher.

HANG TEN AND HANG ON!

One for the "What were they thinking?" file: A twenty-one-year-old man climbed out of the cab of a pickup truck traveling down a Colorado highway and crawled into the truck's bed. He popped up and acted as if he were "surfing the waves" when things took a turn for the worse— by that I mean the driver of the truck took a turn and things couldn't have been worse for the surfer. He was thrown from the truck bed and the highway hotdogger had his final wipeout.

A passenger who allegedly attacked and injured a Continental Airlines ticket agent is suing the airlines for the company's "poor training" of its employees.

THE BUTT OF ALL THE JOKES

Jerry Glenn Nelson had agreed to be the designated driver for the evening and was giving his friend, Jeff Foran, a lift home in his 2000 Dodge Stratus. While they were on Highway 234 along the Arkansas-Oklahoma border near Foreman, Arkansas, a gust of wind blew Foran's cigarette out the window, so he jumped after it. The only problem was that the car was still traveling at 55 to 60 miles per hour. Foran suffered "a substantial case of road rash," mainly on his face, said State Police Trooper Jamie Gravier, in a May 24, 2005, article in the *Texarkana Gazette.* "If anything could make him stop smoking, this should be it." Or maybe the problem isn't his smoking but his drinking.

HIS PARENTS WEREN'T SO CHEERY

Relying on skills learned at a computer game, seven-year-old Perley King of Tacoma, Washington, jumped into his sister's car, and with his pet dog, Bear, drove off in search of his favorite cereal, Cheerios. King drove three miles through busy traffic by alternately hitting the gas pedal and then climbing up on the seat to steer. Instead of getting punished for his actions on April 1, 2000, the boy was given a year's supply of cereal and a new bike by General Mills, the makers of Cheerios, for his "amazing devotion" to their cereal. "So he'll never have to drive to the store again," said General Mills spokeswoman Liv Lane.

"Man's Yard Decoration Flips Drivers the Bird"

—Associated Press headline, December 13, 2002

THE KEY TO SUCCESS

Amanda Webster of London, England, called the Royal Automobile Club when she couldn't get her Ford Focus to start during a shopping trip with her one-year-old son, Oscar. According to a December 3, 2002, article in the *Telegraph*, it soon became evident that the problem was that the aspirin-sized coded radio transponder from her car's key was missing. Since little Oscar had been playing with the keys earlier, he was the prime suspect. Mothers are some of the most ingenious people on the planet, and Webster had the brilliant idea of holding Oscar close to the steering wheel and turning the key in the ignition. The car started right up. Mom and baby made a safe journey back home and eventually the transponder made a safe journey through Oscar's body.

A WING AND A PRAYER

In October 1992, authorities at Barkley Regional Airport in Paducah, Kentucky, reported the bizarre death of an unidentified man who was seen earlier at the airport trying to trade his leather jacket for a ticket to California. The man then tried to hitch a ride on a Northwest Airlines plane by holding on to the wing—when the plane reached an altitude of approximately three hundred feet, the man lost his grip and fell to his death. I think he lost his grip a lot sooner than that.

A one-vehicle crash on the Capital Beltway in Alexandria, Virginia, in April 1999 catapulted Tito, a Chihuahua, over a four-foot concrete median and across four lanes of traffic. He landed safely on the road's grassy shoulder.

Insurance Files
PART EIGHT

The following are actual statements given by insurance policyholders describing automobile accidents in which they were involved.

"The accident happened when the right front door of a car came round the corner without giving a signal."

"No one was to blame for the accident, but it would never have happened if the other driver had been alert."

"I was unable to stop in time and my car crashed into the other vehicle. The driver and passengers then left immediately for a vacation with injuries."

"The pedestrian ran for the pavement, but I got him."

A REAL TRAVEL ADVENTURE

A woman called a travel agent to make reservations, saying, "I want to go from Chicago to Hippopotamus, New York." Needless to say, the agent was rather confused by the request.

"Are you sure that's the name of the town?"

"Yes, I'm sure," said the client. "What flights do you have?"

The agent got on the computer and tried every airport code in the country but couldn't come up with a city named Hippopotamus. She finally got back on the phone and told the person on the other end that she had had no luck locating a city with that name.

"Oh, don't be silly. Everyone knows where it is. Check your map!"

The agent scoured the map of New York state looking for any city that might vaguely sound or look like Hippopotamus. Finally, as a last-ditch effort, she asked the woman, "You don't, by any chance, mean Buffalo, do you?"

"Oh, right, that's it," replied the customer. "I knew it was a big animal."

EVERYONE'S DOING IT

"I can't really answer that question because I don't speak Cuban. It's just a place that I read a long time ago that hijackers were going."

—Curley Lee Compton, when asked why he attempted to hijack a Southwest Airlines plane and fly it to Cuba in February 1991

"Golfer Charged with Drunken Driving"

—Associated Press headline, June 16, 1999

A REAL SCREWUP

In July 1992, the National Transportation Safety Board ruled that the September 1991 crash of a Continental Express commuter plane was due to careless and improper maintenance. The board concluded that while checking the plane's deicer, a Continental inspector had removed forty-seven screws and then failed to replace them or even inform anyone of their removal. The screws held in place the horizontal stabilizing bar, which fell off during the flight and caused the plane to crash.

"Doh! Man Steals GPS Tracking Device"

—*Register* (United Kingdom) headline, September 4, 2003

EXPIRATION DATE

A businessman called his travel agent and wanted to get all the pertinent information for a trip to China. The agent went over all the protocol of getting his passport and shot records, but when he brought up the fact that the man would have to have a visa he was interrupted. "I've been to China before, sir, and I know for a fact that I don't have to have a visa." The agent logged on to his computer and pulled up the requirement for a visit to China and, sure enough, a visa was needed. He got back on the phone and told the man that according to the requirement he had to have a visa. The man shot back, "I'm sorry, pal, but you're wrong. The last time I went to China they accepted my American Express."

Twenty-one-year-old motorcyclist Olivier Faure walked and hitchhiked more than six miles in a state of shock to get to his home from the scene of a horrendous accident. A car had knocked Faure off his motorcycle in the village of Upaix, France, in February 1999, and it wasn't until he was home that he realized his arm had been severed below the elbow.

HAPPY TRAILS TO YOU

While on a class field trip to Washington, D.C., about 40 eighth-grade students from Hartford, Connecticut, were left stranded for a day in May 1996 when their charter bus driver disappeared. Several children reported that the bus driver had picked up a prostitute, who rode on the bus with them. After he dropped the kids off at their hotel around 11 p.m., he drove away with her.

In May 2001, eighteen-year-old Indira Bachoo of Euclid, Florida, had her driving test canceled because, while driving with her mother, she injured a customer after crashing the family car through the front window of the Euclid Post Office.

HEAD OF THE STEERING COMMITTEE

On August 21, 2003, the *Sioux Falls Argus Leader* reported on the driving record of Representative Bill Janklow of South Dakota. Janklow, who was accused of killing a motorcyclist in a collision, claimed that he had to swerve to avoid hitting another vehicle and accidentally struck the motorcycle at an intersection. The newspaper commented that this is the same excuse Janklow used in three previous accidents (one time he had claimed he swerved for an animal), but that in none of the four collisions was there any evidence substantiating the existence of another vehicle or animal.

"Airline Travel Safer Despite More Accidents—Report"

—Reuters headline, January 27, 2000

TOUR-A-LOORA-LOORA

The following, culled from a travel Web site, are official complaints lodged against tour operators in the United Kingdom.

▶ A man complained because no one warned him or his family that there would be fish in the sea.

▶ A angry customer complained because there were far too many Spaniards in Spain.

▶ A tourist complained that the sand at a beach was not the color he had expected: It was not the yellow in the catalog and was simply too white.

THAT CAR'S REALLY SMOKIN'

Twenty-year-old Jonathan Fish had finished smoking a cigarette as he drove across the San Francisco Bay Bridge and flicked the still-lit cigarette out of the window. But the wind blew the cigarette into the backseat of his $30,000 white Ford Expedition SUV, setting it on fire. Fish jumped out of the car without putting it into park and watched helplessly as it started to roll, crashed into a guardrail, and burned down to the frame. According to a February 18, 2005, article in the *San Francisco Chronicle*, Fish was cited by the California Highway Patrol for littering.

FYI ON ATVS

Mourners gathered in Huntington, West Virginia, to pay their final respects to Dustin "Duke" Phillips, who died on July 16, 2005, after he lost control of his all-terrain vehicle and hit a tree. According to Clinton Burley of the Ceredo Volunteer Fire Department, several mourners rode on ATVs to pay special tribute to Phillips, including his sister Maggan, who rode with twenty-year-old Jimmy Spry. Both riders were helmetless when Spry lost control of the ATV he was driving and crashed into a tree. The *Huntington Herald-Dispatch* reported that Spry was hospitalized in fair condition while Ms. Phillips suffered only minor injuries.

"United Plots a Painful Flight Plan"

—Associated Press headline, December 6, 2002

TOUGH DAY AT
THE BODY SHOP

"I thought it was a package that had fallen from a truck," said motorist Mary Ellen Douglas in an interview with the *Dallas Morning News* on July 13, 2005. Douglas was driving on a south Dallas highway when she was forced to swerve around a large item on the road; it wasn't a package—it was a corpse on a gurney. The body of a Louisiana man strapped to a gurney had fallen from the back of a pickup trunk en route to a funeral home in Shreveport, Louisiana, and started rolling down the highway. "The driver of the truck was not aware that he had lost the body," said Dallas police lieutenant Rick Andrews. Then "he went back and retraced his steps and found the body," and continued on his way.

A REAL HANGER-ON

A man on the run from the law tried to evade police by crawling under a parked tractor-trailer in Toronto in March 2006. But the hide-and-seek half-wit picked the wrong truck, because before he could crawl out, the truck started up and headed down Highway 401. A passing motorist noticed the driver was hauling more than he thought and called police. Authorities stopped traffic on the busy highway and arrested the suspended suspected car thief. "I'm amazed that this young man is still alive, to be honest with you," Ontario provincial police constable Joel Doiron said.

"Wife Speeds Off with Naked Man on Car Roof"

—*Wilmington (DE) News Journal* headline, December 4, 2002

AROUND THE WORLD IN SEVEN MINUTES

A very pleasant-sounding woman called an airline asking how it was possible that a flight from Detroit left at 8:20 a.m. and got into Chicago at 8:33 a.m. The ticketing agent tried to explain that Michigan was an hour ahead of Illinois, but that just seemed to confuse the woman even more. After giving up on trying to explain the concept of time zones, the agent finally said, "The plane goes very, very fast." The caller was satisfied with this answer and hung up.

VIOLATION $100.00

Month	Day	Year	City	State

Plate No.	VIN	Expiration date

Name	Location

Clay Sullivan was working security on horseback at the Cheyenne, Wyoming, Frontier Days festival on July 24, 2004, when he began arguing with tow-truck driver Randy LeBeaumont, who had been summoned to remove a car from the parade route. Sullivan thought LeBeaumont was driving his truck down the street during the parade illegally, and when LeBeaumont went back to the cab of his truck to retrieve his cell phone to call the police, Sullivan lassoed him and dragged him 250 feet. Even though the long-legged LeBeaumont was able to stay on his feet and wasn't hurt during the lassoing he was awarded $340,000 by a Wyoming jury in February 2008.

Signature	Officer No.

HANG UP OR
HANG UPSIDE DOWN

"It was unbelievable," said a Portland, Oregon, firefighter. "She's hanging partially out of her vehicle, and she proceeds to have an argument with her husband about where she is." He was referring to the November 1995 scene of an automobile accident in which a woman and her two children were trapped upside down in their Alfa Romeo. The firefighters were using the Jaws of Life tool to free the occupants of the car when the woman asked them to stop making so much noise so she could take a cell phone call from her husband.

"Invisible Man Faked Death in Paddington Rail Crash"

—*Sunday Times* (London), February 6, 2000

THAT SINKING FEELING

In September 1992, twenty-two-year-old David Wayne Godin was returning from his bachelor party when he lost control of his vehicle and plunged into a lake near Dartmouth, Nova Scotia. Authorities determined that Godin might not have drowned had it not been for a wacky party gift his friends had attached to his leg—an actual ball and chain. If they would have given him a battle-ax, he might have been able to cut his way out of his sinking car.

A Turkish truck driver was killed
when he tried to warm up frozen diesel fuel
by lighting a fire under his truck.

AIRLINING THEIR POCKETS

A Dallas, Texas, jury awarded nearly fifteen million dollars to two men who were seriously injured after they smashed into the back of another car at the Dallas Fort Worth International Airport. The car had stopped in traffic to read American Airlines flight information when the two men rear-ended it. The jury justified awarding the men who hit the car, even though they had been following too closely, by stating that they were only 2 percent at fault. The car that was hit, they claimed, was 32 percent at fault, but because they put the signs up in the first place, American Airlines was deemed to be 66 percent at fault. To make matters worse, the jury assessed an additional ten million dollars in punitive damages in the November 1997 case.

ANGORA-PHOBIA

A man from Switzerland was pulled over for going 100 miles per hour in a 60 mile-per-hour zone during a trip through Ontario, Canada. Canadian police spokesman Joel Doiron said the man's excuse for speeding was that he was taking advantage "of the ability to go faster without risking hitting a goat." Doiron, who is a twenty-year veteran of the police force, said he's never seen a goat on the eastern highways of Ontario before. "I've never been to Switzerland, but I guess there must be a lot of goats there," he said. The report from the BBC News on September 7, 2006, said the excuse didn't work, and the man was issued a $330 fine for speeding.

VIOLATION

$100.00

No. 187

Month	Day	Year	City	State

Plate No.	VIN	Expiration date

Name	Location

During a February 2001 funeral procession in Florence, Alabama, a twenty-year-old motorist became angry that he had to wait for the line of mourners in their cars to pass on the highway. The man began yelling obscenities at the funeral procession, and a fistfight broke out after he threw a bottle at a car full of mourners.

Signature	Officer No.

THIS MESSAGE WILL SELF-DESTRUCT . . .

During a British Airways flight from London to Los Angeles in June 1999, four hundred passengers were terrified to hear a prerecorded emergency warning message. The captain had learned how to respond quickly, however, because this was the third month in a row that an emergency message had accidentally been broadcast into the cabin. In April, the first time the problem arose, a message told passengers the plane was about to crash-land into the Atlantic Ocean.

"Kite Takes Flight with Norwegian in Tow"

—*Fresno Bee* headline, December 3, 2002

WHAT GOES UP . . .

According to FAA transcripts published by the *St. Louis Post-Dispatch* on March 5, 2005, two pilots for the regional carrier Pinnacle Airlines told air traffic controllers they were flying at the plane's highest maximum altitude "to have a little fun." The plane, a Canadair CRJ2, with no passengers or other crew on board, was at forty-one thousand feet when both engines shut down. In one of their final communications, the pilots asked whether it was "cool" if they took the plane to a lower altitude to try and restart their engines.

According to a March 9, 2001, article in the *Pittsburgh Post-Gazette*, forty-nine-year-old Dale A. Sunday was discovered in her car on the right-field warning track (the dirt area closest to the wall or fence) at the Pittsburgh Pirates' ballpark, which was still under construction at that time. The only way Sunday could have gotten her car onto the field was through a difficult-to-navigate construction tunnel.

THE BLIND LEADING
THE BLIND

Even though thirty-one-year-old George Edgar Lizarralde was legally blind and had failed the driver's test three times, the Department of Motor Vehicles in Santa Ana, California, issued him a driver's license in 1985. Furthermore, he was granted the license even though he had failed the vision test on the fourth try. During a January 1994 trial, the DMV's negligence was judged the main cause of the accident in which Lizarralde mowed down Deborah Ann Mohr while she crossed the street in a crosswalk in 1990.

"Pilots for Christ Program Provides
a Wing and a Prayer"

—*Raleigh (NC) News and Observer* headline, October 30, 2002

DOUBLE TROUBLE

Twin sisters Cynthia and Crystal Mikota were on a United Airlines flight from San Francisco to Alaska in April 2001 when they began screaming at each other. A flight attendant tried to calm the two twenty-two-year-olds and received a bloody nose from Cynthia. Later in the flight, there was another altercation outside the lavatory, where one or both of the twins had smoked. Eventually one of the pilots got the girls to return to their seats and sat with them to prevent any other outbreaks—but that didn't work. Crystal hit a flight attendant and then jumped on the back of another, putting him in a chokehold while her sister was being placed in flexible handcuffs. The plane was diverted to Anchorage, Alaska, where FBI agents escorted the still-screaming twins off the plane. They were sentenced to up to twenty years in prison.

FLIPPER AND FLIPPER OFF

Nancy Glass, who appeared on the TV magazine shows *Inside Edition* and *American Journal* in the 1980s and '90s, was on vacation in the Bahamas and decided to swim with the dolphins through Dolphin Encounters on Nassau's Blue Lagoon Island. Glass was in the water and signaled one of the five-hundred-pound dolphins to jump over her—which he almost did. According to a December 13, 2002, Associated Press article, the mammal fell short and landed on Glass's head, shoving her underwater. Glass claimed she wasn't warned of any potential risk of swimming with the dolphins and sued Dolphin Encounters, claiming she now suffers neck pain and hearing loss.

"Drunk Horse and Cart Driver Loses License"

—Reuters headline, October 4, 2002

A REAL MOBILE HOME

An Amtrak train loaded with sports fans was hurtling down the tracks in Washington when the conductor looked up and noticed there was something on the tracks—a house! The train smashed into the house, tearing it into small pieces, but fortunately no one was hurt. Moments before the crash, two men were seen on the roof of the house holding up electric wires so they could move the house across the tracks. This is the first example of a house on the wrong side of both tracks.

VIOLATION $100.00

Month	Day	Year	City	State

Plate No.		VIN	Expiration date

Name	Location

A motorist from West Seneca, New York, noticed a small fire under the hood of his car and quickly drove into a self-service car wash in order to douse the flames. According to a May 21, 2003, article in the *Buffalo News,* the man didn't have any quarters to activate the car wash and the fire quickly spread, destroying four of the car wash's eight bays.

Signature   Officer No.

CAN YOU HEAR ME NOW?

Jacqueline Dotson lost control of her SUV while driving near Winchester, Kentucky, forcing several cars off the road before overcompensating and flipping the vehicle over a guardrail. According to a February 3, 2006, report on WLEX-TV in Lexington, it took rescue workers nearly an hour and a half to extricate her from the wreckage using the Jaws of Life. Police suspect that Dotson hadn't been paying full attention to her driving because they found her severed arm—still clutching a cell phone—on the road near the site.

"Italian Plane Passengers See Flames, Vote to Land"

—Reuters headline, March 4, 2002

WALKING ON THIN ICE

As reported on January 28, 2007, by its rival station, WISN-TV in Milwaukee, Wisconsin, a news crew for WDJT-TV, reporting on the danger of thin ice covering Big Muskego Lake, drove onto the lake and fell through. No one was injured during the accident, but the hugely expensive high-tech van was ruined—and the competition scooped the story.

According to an article in the *Myrtle Beach (SC) Sun News*, on August 21, 2003, a car traveling in the early morning hours on Interstate 77 just north of Charlotte, North Carolina, was struck by a flying speedboat. The boat was traveling at a high rate of speed across Lake Norman, which runs adjacent to the interstate, became airborne, bounced off the car, and landed in the median.

WHERE THERE'S SMOKE . . .

John Ferrell was seriously burned on April 8, 2007, when an explosion in the back of his pickup truck caught the vehicle on fire. Montgomery County, Tennessee, sheriff's office spokesman Ted Denny said investigators of the accident concluded that the explosion started in the grill. Not the grille on the front of the truck but the barbeque grill Ferrell had put in the truck's bed. "Apparently, when he loaded up the grill he still had hot charcoals, which somehow got too close to the propane tank, and it exploded," Denny said. "Obviously, we would urge people not to drive with burning grills in their vehicles." Ferrell was taken by helicopter to Vanderbilt University Medical Center for burn treatment.

The Associated Press reported on August 27, 2003, that a man had lost control of his car and died when he crashed into the O. R. Woodyard Funeral Home.

I GET BY WITH A LITTLE HELP FROM MY FRIENDS

Abbotsford, Wisconsin, police were temporarily confused when they pulled over a 1985 Chevrolet truck for reckless driving and found two Dorchester, Wisconsin, men in the driver's area (and, no, they weren't doing anything nasty). According to a *Marshfield News-Herald* article from August 28, 2007, Harvey J. Miller, who has no legs, was steering the truck while Edwin Marzinske was on the floorboard operating the pedals. Both men were issued citations for drunken driving and driving after their licenses had been revoked. A third man, who was also drunk but did have his legs, used them to walk home after the incident.

MEN ARE FROM MARS

A forty-two-year-old Frenchman raced through a roadblock on the A55 motorway in Marseille, France, prompting a high-speed chase by police that eventually ended in a minor crash. When the man was in police custody, he confided that the reason he ran the roadblock was that he was being chased by Martians. The man passed a Breathalyzer test for alcohol after the December 30, 2002, incident, but police detained him for further drug tests and a psychiatric evaluation.

"Girls Slam on Brakes after Spotting Skid Marks"

—Associated Press headline, September 30, 2004

AND NEVER THE TRAIN SHALL MEET

"There are all kinds of ways to get distracted these days," said Eugene, Oregon, police spokeswoman Kerry Delf. "We don't recommend any of them while you're driving." She was referring to the case of thirty-eight-year-old Robert Gillespie, who, while text messaging someone on his cell phone, looked up to see a Union Pacific freight train crossing in front of him ("OMG!"). According to an October 18, 2007, article in the *Portland Oregonian*, rescue workers pried Gillespie, who was still conscious, out of the crushed vehicle, and he was sent to the hospital with non-life-threatening injuries.

"Patrol Car Hit by Flying Outhouse"

—*Milwaukee Journal Sentinel*, October 3, 2003

STUCK IN THE MAYER

"I've pulled out a lot of vehicles," said Dave Kurzejewski of Costy's Truck and Auto Mart. "But that's the first wiener I've ever pulled out." Kurzejewski was talking frankly about being called by Mansfield, New York, police to pull the stuck Oscar Mayer Wienermobile from a snow-covered highway. Emily Volpini and Caylen Goudie, the two hotdoggers who were driving when the Wienermobile went off the road on February 10, 2008, were unhurt but didn't relish the idea of getting out in the cold to wait for the tow truck.

According to a November 2, 2003, article in the *Boston Globe*, a twenty-year-old woman died in a single-car accident in Bridgewater, Massachusetts, after she lost control of her car while talking on her cell phone on Route 106 and crashed into a Cingular Wireless store.

AIRHEADS

In September 1995, U.S. Army General Joseph Ashy was reassigned from his post in Naples, Italy, to his new position in Colorado Springs, Colorado. Instead of Ashy taking a commercial flight to Colorado, a Lockheed C-141 Starlifter with a crew of thirteen was deployed from New Jersey, flew to Italy to pick up the general and his aide, and then flew them to Colorado Springs—costing taxpayers an estimated $120,000. The C-141 Starlifter was designed for strategic airlifts and is capable of carrying up to seventy thousand pounds of equipment and supplies, 154 troops, or 123 fully equipped paratroopers, but during this flight the only passengers were Ashy and his aide.

"Nude Vacations Rise Despite Flaccid Industry"

—MSN.com, January 4, 2003

LET MY PEOPLE GO!

An employee in the wardrobe department at Universal Studios in Hollywood was driving through different back lots in July 1994 when she became disoriented and lost her way. The thirty-two-year-old woman decided to follow a tram carrying visitors in the hope that the driver would eventually lead her to a place she recognized. The tram, however, was headed into the "Red Sea" attraction, in which the waters are "parted" while the tram drives though and then released. The woman wasn't following close enough and was engulfed by the ensuing waters—she was stuck in the small lake for nearly an hour before firefighters could rescue her.

"Survey Finds Dirtier Subways after Cleaning Jobs Were Cut"

—*New York Times*, November 22, 1995

HOOLIGANS WIN!

The *Irish Times* reported in February 1992 about a recently won lawsuit filed by thirty-eight Irish soccer fans against two independent Italian bus companies. The lawsuit claimed that the bus drivers were at fault for making them miss the 1990 World Cup games in Italy. They testified that the bus drivers purposely drove inordinately slow (averaging only 20 miles per hour) on two trips, making the fans miss one game and then later missing the ferry that would have taken them to another game.

VIOLATION $100.00

No. 207

Month	Day	Year	City	State

Plate No.	VIN	Expiration date

Name	Location

The *Inland Valley (CA) Daily Bulletin* reported on October 31, 2000, that a twenty-nine-year-old man who was using a flashlight to substitute for his faulty headlights on his ATV accidentally drove over a cliff.

Signature	Officer No.

TWO FOR ONE

A sixty-seven-year-old woman lost control of her car while driving in Houston, Texas, and was killed after crashing into the lead car of a funeral procession about to depart Guadalupe Funeral Home for a cemetery. According to a May 24, 2006, article in the *Houston Chronicle*, the family of the newly departed woman announced that they would go ahead and leave her body at Guadalupe for funeral arrangements.

Local law in Cicero, Illinois, states that any vehicle used during the solicitation of prostitution is subject to confiscation even if, as the *Chicago Sun-Times* reported on July 13, 2003, the vehicle is a municipal transit bus that the driver was returning after his shift.

TECHNOLOGY WITHOUT AN INTERESTING NAME

Matt Brownlee, considered a recidivist drunken driver, was acquitted of criminal DUI charges in Ottawa, Ontario, according to a March 28, 2006, report from the Canadian Broadcasting Corporation. Psychiatrists concluded that the thirty-three-year-old man's latest accident stemmed from a brain injury he sustained in a 1996 accident, in which he believed Shania Twain was helping drive his car. (Brownlee has a psychiatric disorder that makes him believe he is in telepathic communication with celebrities.)

"Jury Clears Cow in Car Accident"

—Associated Press headline, February 1, 2004

BLACK DIAMOND AND BLACK ASPHALT

On January 29, 2007, Miami, Florida's WPLG-TV reported that twenty-two-year-old Jonathas Mendonca was in critical condition in a Fort Lauderdale hospital after "skiing"—holding onto the rear bumper of a car while wearing skates or riding a skateboard—while the vehicle was traveling at 65 miles per hour on Interstate 95.

London's *Daily Telegraph* reported on September 2, 2003, that British brain surgeon Donald Campbell had crashed his twin-engine plane into a house after it had run out of fuel. The article explained that Campbell, who suffered head injuries as a result of the accident, had miscalculated the amount of fuel when he attempted to convert gallons to liters.

A JUNKER OF A DIFFERENT SORT

Ann Biglin of West Yarmouth, Massachusetts, told police that the cause of her single-car accident in February 2007 was because "several old coffee cups" and "assorted pieces of trash" had fallen and hit the accelerator. Police investigating the accident, in which her car jumped a curb and knocked over a light post, determined that it wasn't as simple as she had claimed. They found her car filled at least chest-high with all types of trash. The February 11, 2007, edition of the *Boston Herald* showed a photograph of Biglin's car and described the mess as "mountains of trash" that crashed down like an "avalanche" on her gas pedal.

OWLS WELL THAT ENDS WELL

Trying to cash in on the pet owl craze created by the Harry Potter series, twenty-three-year-old Jason Denton stole Addy, a barn owl, from her owners and tried to take wing. But Addy's cage wouldn't fit into Denton's stolen Ford Fiesta, so he turned the owl free in his car and drove off with it. Soon, however, the owl started clawing and pecking at Denton, who finally rolled down the window and struggled to throw the bird out. According to an article in the August 11, 2007, edition of the *Guardian*, Denton lost control of his car as he was trying to control the owl and wound up crashing. He was charged with burglary and treated for scratches and bites. Addy was safely recovered and returned to Hogwarts . . . I mean, her owners.

ALL GASSED UP AND READY TO GO

Two teenage girls from Cleveland, Ohio, ran away from home, and one brought her pet dog, Bambi, with her. They boarded a bus headed for Minneapolis and told the driver that Bambi was a "guide dog." The girls, aged twelve and thirteen, overfed Bambi during the trip and the dog got a noxious case of flatulence. According to a February 15, 2006, article in the *Cleveland Plain Dealer*, the dog's gas was so bad that it started a commotion on the bus, and when police investigated they discovered the two runaways.

According to an April 25, 2007, Associated Press article, the director of the Feline Health Center at Cornell University, a prominent cat veterinarian, was killed near Marathon, New York, when he lost control of his motorcycle when a cat crossed the road.

FLY ME TO THE MOON . . .

A woman called her local travel agency requesting information on planning an upcoming trip to Cape Town. The agent started giving her all the information on the length of the flight, price, and passport information. When he got to the part about passports, the woman stopped him. "I'm not trying to make you look stupid," she said. "But Cape Town is in Massachusetts." The travel agent, who is, by his very trade, extremely familiar with the locations of cities and countries, said, "I'm sorry, but Cape Cod is in Massachusetts; Cape Town is in South Africa." The woman responded by quickly slamming down her phone.

According to a December 17, 2007, article in the *New York Post*, the New Jersey Turnpike Authority filed a lawsuit against the families of four people killed by a tractor-trailer that had lost control in 2006. The suit demanded an unknown sum of money from the victims' families, presumably to recover cleanup costs and damage-repair expenses to the roadway. However, the lawsuit was immediately withdrawn after a reporter for the *New York Post* asked NJTA lawyer William Ziff for a comment.

SNAKING THROUGH TRAFFIC

Charles Page was driving down Golden Gate Parkway in Naples, Florida, when he noticed a man in another car struggling with what looked like a rope around his neck. Thirty-year-old Courtland Page Johnson was actually fighting his four-foot boa constrictor, which was coiled around his neck and had bit his face. After he had banged into several roadside barricades, Johnson jumped out of his PT Cruiser, untangled himself from the snake, and then quickly slithered away. Police located Johnson after the March 28, 2006, accident at his house. He was arrested and charged with leaving the scene of a crash and taken to the Naples Jail Center.

HIS OWN WORST ENEMY

After a city dump truck smashed his car, Curtis Gokey of Lodi, California, sued city hall for $3,600. You may not be surprised that someone would sue the city in a case like this until you find out that the driver of the dump truck was Gokey himself. Gokey admitted that he was the one driving the truck but still felt that he was entitled to be compensated for the damage to his own car. The city refused his claim. Gokey's wife, Rhonda, then tried to sue the city and even upped the price to $4,800, but she was told that one spouse can't sue the other "for damage to community property." According to an Associated Press article from March 16, 2006, the city council denied her claim, too.

"Man Charged for Trying to MacGyver Propane Tank to Car Engine"

—London *(Ontario, Canada) Free Press* headline, February 15, 2007

GOING IN CIRCLES

Carleen Jordan, a recently hired newspaper delivery truck driver in Clinton Township, Michigan, jumped out of her truck to restock a store's newspaper racks and accidentally put the vehicle in reverse. The truck took off and circled the area wildly for twenty minutes in August 2007, smashing into cars and crushing mailboxes, before police were able to stop it with spike strips.

According to an April 13, 2007, article in the *London Daily Mail*, Andrew Workman accidentally crashed his car into another in Shepley, West Yorkshire, in England, after he lost control of his car when a bee flew through the window and stung him in the crotch.

IT'S BIG—BUT IT AIN'T THAT BIG!

A man on a business trip called his travel agent and wanted to make sure he could get a rental car in Dallas, Texas. When the agent pulled up the man's reservations she noticed that he had only a one-hour layover in Dallas and asked him why he needed a car. The man explained, "I heard Dallas was a big airport, and I need a car to drive between the gates to save time."

London's High Court approved an insurance settlement in March 2007 for the equivalent of roughly $2.4 million for motorcyclist Kunal Lindsay, who was struck by an automobile in 2002. After extensive physical therapy, Lindsay noted that he had become uncontrollably and chronically horny and had acquired an unhealthy attraction to cell phones. London's *Daily Telegraph* reported on March 2, 2007, that the court was convinced that the accident had caused these conditions, which, because of Lindsay's constant nagging of his wife for sex, led to the breakup of Lindsay's marriage.

PUNCHING HIS TICKET

A thirty-three-year-old man, identified only as Smits, was beaten to death by five so-called controllers from a local bus company in Riga, Latvia, in January 1994. Local police confirmed that controllers routinely beat people they believe to be riding illegally, and when Smits couldn't produce his bus ticket they assumed he was a stowaway.

VIOLATION $100.00

No. 225

Month	Day	Year	City	State

Plate No.	VIN	Expiration date

Name	Location

On July 26, 2007, television station WSB in Atlanta reported that a twenty-four-year-old woman was killed while trying to get into a gated parking lot in Lawrenceville, Georgia. The woman had leaned out of her window to insert a key card into a gate-opening kiosk when her car lurched forward, pinning her head between the kiosk and the car. Police investigators said the woman hadn't put the car into park.

Signature	Officer No.

ROSA PARKS WOULD SCREAM

School bus driver Leon Hayes was reprimanded in June 1992 by Laidlaw Transit, Inc., which oversaw his Seattle bus route. Hayes faced disciplinary retribution after he was caught charging students between fifty cents and one dollar for the honor of sitting in the highly sought after seats in the back of the bus.

"When he's sober, he's very much against drinking and driving."

—Attorney for the founder of Students Against Drinking and Driving at
Calgary University (Canada), in response to his client's second drunken driving offense

NOT A REQUEST STOP

Dawne Hamblin, a shuttle bus driver for the elderly and disabled, left her bus to help a young girl who had been hit by an automobile. Hamblin comforted the girl, directed traffic around the accident, and stayed by her side until an ambulance arrived. Shortly after the January 1992 incident, Hamblin was informed by the owners of the Milwaukee, Wisconsin, shuttle service that her actions would not go unnoticed. Hamblin was fired from her job because, according to management, she had disobeyed instructions from her dispatcher by stopping and helping the injured girl.

"I can't help it, officer. Someone has hypnotized me to park illegally."

—Excuse offered up by the driver of illegally parked car

DRIVING IS NOT HIS RACKET

Robert Kadera of Lake Villa, Illinois, knew his teenage son was running late for a tennis date and that it would take them at least forty-five minutes to drive there, so he thought they would wing it—in his four-seat 1949 Piper Clipper airplane. But it wasn't the flight that eventually got the sixty-five-year-old electrical engineer into trouble; it was the landing at a golf course across the street from the tennis complex. "We're all pretty dumbfounded," said Lincolnshire police chief Randy Melvin. "I don't have any idea what the guy was thinking. He was going to park his plane across the street like nobody would notice." Kadera promised to drive the next time.

"Man Run Over by Freight Train Dies"

—*Los Angeles Times*, March 2, 1995

TEST-OSTERONE

A thirty-year-old Australian man convinced a car dealer in Melbourne to let him test-drive a Honda Accord, and it tested the limits of the police's imagination. The man took the $37,000 car on a six-day, 1,988-mile test drive. "He drove from Melbourne to Adelaide to Alice Springs," Tennant Creek police constable James Gray-Spence told Reuters in a March 7, 2008, article. A roadblock was set up to capture the man after he failed to pay for gasoline on the last leg of his test-drive. He was arrested and charged with possession of stolen property and aggravated unlawful use of a motor vehicle. So the question is, did the man pass or fail his test-drive?

THE SLOW WHEELS
OF JUSTICE

Tomas Delgado was driving in excess of 100 miles per hour in a 55 mile-per-hour zone in August 2004 near Haro, Spain, when he collided with and killed a seventeen-year-old bicyclist. Two years later, Delgado sued the family of the deceased boy for twenty-nine thousand dollars for damages to his car. According to a January 30, 2008, Associated Press article, Delgado finally dropped the lawsuit in January 2008, possibly because of the enormous amount of bad press he was receiving.

Insurance Files
PART NINE

The following are actual statements given by insurance policyholders describing automobile accidents in which they were involved.

"I saw her look at me twice. She appeared to be making slow progress when we met on impact."

Q: Could either driver have done anything to avoid the accident?

A: Traveled by bus?

The claimant had collided with a cow. The questions and answers on the claim form included the following:

Q: What warning was given by you?

A: Horn.

Q: What warning was given by the other party?

A: Moo.

SLOW-SPEED CHASE

A call came into a Toronto police department warning officers that a man driving a backhoe was heading toward a car wash, apparently with the intention of knocking down a portion of the wall in order to get at the facility's coin machine. The call came in from a vehicle that had left its intended route in order to chase the would-be robber. According to a February 13, 2008, article in the *Toronto Star*, the vehicle that was pursuing the backhoe was a snowplow.

"Norwegian Motorist Is Slapped with Parking Ticket While Stuck in Traffic Jam"

—Associated Press headline, September 3, 2004

IT'LL GET YOU THERE AND BACK

As reported in an October 15, 2007, Associated Press article, a sixty-one-year-old Beckley, West Virginia, man was detained by police at the King Tut Drive-In for taking his four grandchildren to a movie. It wasn't the type of movie he took them to see that was the problem, nor was the man intoxicated. He was questioned as to why he had driven his grandchildren, all around age four, on a busy street in a fifteen-foot motorboat pulled by a lawnmower. The grandfather seemed unaware that he had placed the children in danger, even though the vehicle was unregistered and the children were not in proper seat restraints. The good news is that the drive-in is now nicely trimmed.

IF AT FIRST YOU DON'T SUCCEED . . .

According to a December 3, 2007, article in the *Deseret (UT) Morning News*, a seventy-three-year-old woman was accidentally killed in Ogden, Utah, when a motor home ran over her. It was not clear to investigators whether the woman had died when she was first run over or when the driver backed up to see what he had run over and crushed the woman again.

The *St. Petersburg (FL) Times* reported on May 10, 2006, that thirty-year-old Lance Kocses was given a citation by police for causing a five-thousand-dollar accident in Seminole, Florida. Officers investigating the accident said Kocses was distracted while attempting to make a left turn because he was eating a bowl of Frosted Flakes.

EVERYONE'S YELLOW ON THIS BUS

School bus driver Robert Horton, twenty-two, and his friend had child endangerment charges filed against them in Mineola, New York, in September 1996. Was Horton driving recklessly? Were he and his friend drunk? Nope. According to police, the two men were charged because they had told scary stories to their five- and six-year-old passengers.

VIOLATION

$100.00

No. 237

Month	Day	Year	City	State
Plate No.		VIN		Expiration date
Name		Location		

New York's *Newsday* newspaper reported on January 31, 2006, that motorist Stephen Nielsen was finally stopped by Suffolk County police after they spotted him going 40 miles per hour on the Long Island Expressway sound asleep with his eyes closed and his mouth opened.

Signature

Officer No.

OPTIONAL EQUIPMENT EXTRA

"It came with the car when I bought it," was the excuse given by a drunken driving suspect in Redondo Beach, California, in October 1996. The arresting officer, Joseph Fonteno, became suspicious after he saw the man's white Mazda driving down the Pacific Coast Highway with half of a traffic-light pole, complete with lights, lying across the car's hood.

While visiting Bedford Hills, New York, a computer technician from Silicon Valley adhered to his car's global positioning system so trustingly that he wound up on the tracks of the Metro-North train. Unfortunately, the man's car stalled on the tracks, but he was able to bail out of the car shortly before the train obliterated it.

MAP QUEST

During a visit to Miami, Bret Lauritzen ignored his wife, Christine's, directions and the couple wound up in a bad section of town. The Tacoma, Washington, couple was robbed, and Christine suffered a severe injury to her arm. In 1992, Christine filed a lawsuit for negligence against her husband, claiming that had Bret listened to her directions they wouldn't have been robbed and she wouldn't have been injured.

The *Metro*, a London newspaper, reported the death of a train driver in Berlin, Germany. Apparently, while the train was going 70 miles per hour, the driver needed to answer the call of nature, leaned too far out of the train door, and fell to his death.

THEY ALL LOOK ALIKE TO ME

A seventy-seven-year-old Jacksonville, Florida, man decided to help out his busy daughter by riding his bicycle to Long Branch Elementary School to pick up his four-year-old grandson. When he arrived back home, instead of getting an "Atta boy" from his daughter, he got a "Who's that boy?" The grandfather had picked up a boy and put him on his bike without ever realizing he had the wrong child. According to a November 8, 2007, report, the mother of the boy who was accidentally taken exclaimed, "[The two boys] don't even look alike."

HOUSTON, WE HAVE A PROBLEM

Joseph Seidl and Michael Sullivan thought they had come up with a foolproof way of disposing of an illegal cache of methamphetamine if they were ever pulled over by the police. The two men obviously weren't rocket scientists, so why they chose a four-foot rocket, with the two pounds of drugs stashed inside, is anyone's guess. According to the Missouri Highway Patrol, the rocket, which was set up in the trunk of their car, was wired to a switch in the front. When the switch was activated, the trunk would pop open, the rocket would rotate into a vertical position, and away would go the incriminating evidence. When trooper Tommy Wally pulled the pair over in Callaway County, Seidl and Sullivan thought it would be "one giant leap for mankind" and quickly flipped the switch. But they forgot one thing—to plug the rocket into the car's cigarette lighter. The *Columbia Tribune* reported in August 6, 2006, that Seidl and Sullivan pleaded guilty to conspiracy to distribute methamphetamine. Why were they pulled over in the first place, you might ask? They were speeding. Of course, they were speeding—they were delivering methamphetamine.

TIME TO CHANGE THE BABY OIL

"When officers arrived, she was still caring for the baby," a California Highway Patrol spokesman said. Apparently an unnamed seventeen-year-old girl was startled when she heard a cry from her baby, lost control of her car, and crashed on a freeway near Pleasanton. The girl was unharmed but was charged with driving without a license, and the baby was eventually deactivated. The "baby" was an educational doll given to her in school, according to a December 2006 article in the *Contra Costa Times*, and programmed to cry when it needed to be fed, changed, or comforted.

VIOLATION

$100.00

Month	Day	Year	City	State
Plate No.		VIN		Expiration date
Name		Location		

The Hackensack, New Jersey, newspaper, the *Record*, reported on an eighty-one-year-old school crossing guard who was accidentally run over and killed in Park Ridge, New Jersey, by a seventy-year-old crossing guard who was driving to his own post.

Signature	Officer No.

A REAL BLIND CURVE

The HOV (High Occupancy Vehicle) lane is intended to encourage carpooling, and the police have heard a lot of excuses from people who violate the law by driving solo—people like Sherman Hill, who was charged with evading police and driving in an HOV lane outside San Francisco. Hill told a judge he wasn't alone in his car when he was arrested in 1990 because his seeing-eye dog was in the front seat with him. Hill claimed to be blind in his left eye and partially blind in the right and that his dog is trained to bark when he gets too close to another car. Why did he speed up when the patrolman hit his sirens? Because, Hill explained, he was trying to cool down his dog. The judge didn't believe the shaggy dog story, and Hill was found guilty on both charges.

I'M WARNING YOU

Thirty-six-year-old Michele Rardin told patrolman Randy Komisarcik in July 1993 that the reason she was driving 80 miles per hour in Hebron, Indiana, was that the oil-warning indicator light on her dashboard came on and she was trying to race home "before the car blew up."

$100.00

No. 248

Month	Day	Year	City	State

Plate No.		VIN		Expiration date

Name	Location

A judge had a hard time believing the excuse offered up by a man accused of allowing his automobile to lunge forward, nearly hitting a police officer, during a traffic stop. The man claimed that he wasn't driving the car at the time, and he blamed his two dogs. He said one dog was pressing the gas pedal, and then the other dog put the car into gear.

Signature	Officer No.

THE BIG BANG THEORY

In September 1996, Paul and Bonnie Stiller were driving around at 2 a.m. in Andover Township, New Jersey, when things suddenly turned explosive. It wasn't an argument that lit their fuse; it was the fact that they had lit the fuse on a quarter stick of dynamite that they intended to throw out of the window. Their plan backfired when the dynamite bounced off their window, which was rolled up, and exploded in their car. The dynamite duo, who claimed they were simply bored, blew themselves straight to the hospital.

Born in April 1993 in Little Rock, Arkansas:
Miss Lexus Camry Peterson

HEY MOTHER TRUCKER

"I just looked down briefly on the floor where I had thrown a couple of doughnuts I was going to eat later, to see where they had landed," recalled semitruck driver Merv Bontrager. Bontrager was so distracted by the doughnuts that he lost control of his rig, it started tipping, and "I couldn't bring it back [upright]," he said. According to a May 20, 2007, Associated Press article, his truck flipped near Minot, North Dakota, spilling his load of seed.

"Forty-Two Injured in Four-Taxi Pileup"

—Associated Press headline, November 23, 2004

KEEP ON TRUCKIN'

In June 2007, the Michigan State Police received a number of bizarre emergency calls regarding a semitruck pushing a man in a wheelchair down Red Arrow Highway in Paw Paw, Michigan. It turned out that the calls were valid. Troopers discovered that twenty-one-year-old Ben Carpenter, seat-belted in his wheelchair, had been pushed nearly two miles at speeds of up to 50 miles per hour by a truck whose driver had no idea what was going on. Apparently, when the truck accidentally struck Carpenter, the handles on his wheelchair became stuck in the grille and he was taken on the ride of his life. Amazingly, Carpenter survived the ordeal completely unscathed and even said he enjoyed the experience. "It was like a ride at a fair," Carpenter said later.

LUCKY AS CRAP

An automobile accident in Augusta, Georgia, caused a car to burst into flames, and it quickly became engulfed. The driver was killed, and it is likely that the passenger would have died in the June 2007 fire, too, if it weren't for a lucky intervention. A pump truck from a local plumbing company that had just finished a septic tank–cleaning job was passing by at the time, and the driver quickly dumped 1,500 gallons of raw sewage onto the car, extinguishing the flames and saving the life of the car's passenger.

"Snippy Flight Attendant Felt Prodded to Poke"

—St. Petersburg (FL) Times headline, January 17, 2004